THE WOUNDED WARRIOR

DR. STEVE STEPHENS

Multnomah® Publishers *Sisters, Oregon*

THE WOUNDED WARRIOR

published by Multnomah Publishers, Inc.

© 2006 by Dr. Steve Stephens

Published in association with Van Diest Literary Agency

International Standard Book Number: 1-59052-705-4

Cover design by The DesignWorks Group, Inc.

Unless otherwise indicated, Scripture quotations are from:

Holy Bible, New Living Translation
© 1996. Used by permission of Tyndale House Publishers, Inc.
All rights reserved.

Other Scripture quotations are from:

The Holy Bible, New International Version (NIV)
© 1973, 1984 by International Bible Society,
used by permission of Zondervan Publishing House

The Message
© 1993, 1994, 1995, 1996, 2000, 2001, 2002
Used by permission of NavPress Publishing Group

New American Standard Bible® (NASB) © 1960, 1977, 1995
by the Lockman Foundation. Used by permission.

The Living Bible (TLB)
© 1971. Used by permission of Tyndale House Publishers, Inc.
All rights reserved.

Multnomah is a trademark of Multnomah Publishers, Inc.,
and is registered in the U.S. Patent and Trademark Office.
The colophon is a trademark of Multnomah Publishers, Inc.

Printed in the United States of America

Library of Congress Cataloging-in-Publication Data

Stephens, Steve.

The wounded warrior / Steve Stephens.
    p. cm.
  ISBN 1-59052-705-4
  1. Men--Religious life. 2. Psychic trauma--Religious aspects--Christianity. 3.
Spiritual healing. I. Title.
  BV4528.2.S69 2006
  248.8'6--dc22

                                        2006013618

For information:
MULTNOMAH PUBLISHERS, INC.
601 N. LARCH ST.
SISTERS, OREGON 97759

06 07 08 09 10—10 9 8 7 6 5 4 3 2 1 0

CONTENTS

BLEEDING ON THE BEACH

I WAS IN SHOCK.

I stood at the edge of the ocean and stared at the waves for hours. I never knew I could hurt so much. If it had been physical pain, I could have clenched my teeth and dealt with it. But this was an emotional pain from a wound that had torn my heart in two, shattered my spirit, and left me aching in ways I never thought possible. I wanted to cry out to God, but my voice was hollow. Besides God was gone. He had betrayed and abandoned me.

I had never felt so alone.

I was twenty-one years old and my life felt like it was over.

I stood on that beach broken, empty, hopeless. *So what do I do now?* I asked myself. *Should I live or die?* I didn't know. I didn't care. I just stood there, watching the waves as the sun set and darkness surrounded me. It seemed to swallow me and make me invisible. Somehow this seemed quite appropriate. Then came the rain. It began as a sprinkle—a light, warm drizzle. I didn't move. I just waited. I didn't know what I was waiting for. I just waited.

A wind slapped me in the face and then the drops came in earnest—big, sloppy, pregnant drops that soaked through my sweatshirt and made me shiver. The rain ran down my face and I wiped it from my eyes. The shower persisted and I finally grew tired of nature's outburst. Only my feet were still dry as I went home, stripped off my wet clothing, and fell into bed. *Maybe tomorrow will be better.*

The next morning the sun rose, but the world was cloaked in a low-hanging fog. I couldn't see more than five feet in front of me. I didn't feel like doing anything, but something inside me urged me to breathe deep and give it a try. So I stepped out of my house and launched into a lifestyle of walking through the motions; I talked and ate and smiled and read and worked. On the outside, all looked normal. On the inside I was a wounded warrior who daily bound up his injuries and marched resolutely forward, battered and bleeding.

It was hard. It hurt. It was deliberate determination. Each step—one foot in front of the other—was an intentional, specific, gut-wrenching choice. Most of the time I didn't know where I was going. Most of the time I didn't feel like going anywhere. But every day I took steps. On some days I walked far; on others I hardly moved. But I kept stepping forward.

Only after a year did I notice that I was feeling better. By then I had taken a lot of steps and learned a lot of lessons. The wound was still there, but my healing had begun. During the day I started to discover oases of hope and laughter. At night the shadows returned, but they were not as dark as they had once been. I didn't have to hide from them anymore. I could stare at them, smile, and even appreciate them. They had become my friends and teachers. Through my difficult time I had learned one of the most important lessons of my life: *Wounds can make you or break you. It's not the deepness of the wound that kills you; it's your refusal to face reality and step forward.*

Life is full of battles, and every warrior is going to sustain his share of injuries. Some soldiers incur one significant, over-powering wound; others receive numerous minor wounds. Regardless of his past history or present circumstances, every man has his gashes and broken bones.

Deep or superficial. Recent or ancient. Hidden or blatantly obvious. Wounds come in myriad shapes and sizes, but they all have one thing in common. *Pain.*

We all deal with pain differently. Some linger in it too long—absorbed, anxious, or angry. Others try to ignore it, look-ing for distractions from their feelings. Still others get stuck—confused and overwhelmed by surging emotions.

STAGNATION OR ANTICIPATION?

We all seek strategies for dealing with our wounds, the accompanying pain, and the soul-deep scars they leave behind. And we are creative about it; many are the methods we explore. But beware. Some strategies will, in reality, make your struggle toward health more difficult. These bad coping techniques actually intensify the pain and prolong the battle. Here are a few:

- *I'm not wounded.* (Denial)
- *I won't talk about my wounds.* (Shame and isolation)
- *My wounds reduce who I am and what I can accomplish.* (Identity sabotage)
- *God did this to me.* (Blame)
- *I won't seek help; I can do it myself.* (Pride)
- *Nobody can help me.* (Hopelessness)
- *If God cared, He wouldn't have let this happen.* (Playing the orphan)

These thought patterns are not healthy. They can endow your wounds with more power than they warrant. Your wounds need not weaken or destroy you. On the contrary, they can be life-realigning, strength-building checkpoints, for they force us to turn to the inexhaustible source of all strength. It's especially in these times that we must remember the apostle Paul's amazing affirmation: "God can do anything…far more than you could ever imagine or guess or request in your wildest dreams" (Ephesians 3:20, The Message).

We cannot change the past, no matter how hard we try. All of our past hurts, injustices, disappointments, and tragedies have slipped into history, beyond our control. Even so, it is within our power to control something about the present: We can change how we view the painful realities that have touched our lives. We can decide what we say to ourselves about them.

You may find this difficult to accept, but *you have more control over your present situation than you think*. You have the power to believe in a faithful, forward-looking God. The prophet Jeremiah describes the source of your present power: "'I know the plans I have for you,' says the LORD. 'They are plans for good and not for disaster, to give you a future and a hope'" (Jeremiah 29:11).

Every wounded warrior has reason for great hope. God strengthens and empowers. Pain need not defeat or diminish you. Any man, regardless of the severity or extent of his wound, can have a successful, meaningful—even joyful—life.

God has strong hands. He can comfort and heal you. He can use your wounds to lead you into more exciting and fulfilling days than you ever imagined possible. Jesus said, "I came that they may have life, and have it abundantly" (John 10:10, NASB). Your life might not be easy, problem-free, or painless, but it can abound.

BATTALION OF THE BRUISED

You are not alone. We all walk through life with wounds. Unfortunately, we guys tend to keep our mouths shut and suffer in silence. We don't want to air our dirty laundry or expose our soft underbelly. We strap on our armor and hide our hurts, but our outward show of self-possession is a lie.

For some the wound is just a *scratch*—it stings, but it doesn't sideline you. For some it's a *scar*—it reminds you of a long-past battle, maybe internally resolved, maybe not. Your wound could be a *scab*—it covers a fresh injury that is in the process of healing—no problem as long as no one bumps it or picks at it. For others it may be a *sore*—it is tender and raw, with sharp, shooting pain that constantly reminds you of its presence.

This world is home to millions of wounded warriors. Other men's circumstances and surroundings may be vastly different from yours, but pain is pain. This vast company is your band of brothers; we're all fellow soldiers. Each man has a story to tell; many stories may seem surprisingly familiar to you. I will tell some of these stories and explore some of the challenges unique to each masculine injury. Everybody deals with his wounds in his own way, at his own pace. Yet together we will learn a few universal lessons for transforming a wounded warrior into a successful soldier. A victor, maybe even a hero.

God never promised to protect us from all wounds, but He did promise to stand by us and to help us win the fight.

CHAPTER 1
HARD TIMES HAPPEN

APRIL 26, 2003, started out as a normal day.

Aron Ralston, a twenty-seven-year-old climbing expert, drove his pickup truck to a remote place outside Canyonlands National Park in southeastern Utah. Then he rode his mountain bike fifteen miles to begin his climb in a rugged, narrow canyon. It was supposed to be an easy Saturday adventure, but it turned out to be much more than he expected.

After climbing for a few hours, he was reaching for a handhold when an eight-hundred-pound boulder shifted, dropping two feet and crushing his right arm. Aron was trapped more than seventy feet above the canyon floor. The pain was excruciating. He needed help, but he knew there was nobody within miles.

Aron knew that in order to survive he had to keep his head and try to move the boulder. He applied ropes and anchors and brute strength, but the rock would not budge. Night fell, and the temperature dropped to near freezing. Aron wasn't sure whether he was shivering from panic or pain or cold.

The next morning he reconsidered his situation: He could do nothing but wait.

That day he ran out of food. On Tuesday he ran out of water. On Wednesday he could smell his own flesh rotting. If something didn't happen quickly, Aron knew he would die.

On Thursday morning he decided upon drastic action. With his free left hand he tied a tourniquet around his right arm. From his shorts pocket he produced a small knife. Then with a gritty, mind-boggling determination he focused his attention and methodically cut off his right arm. Then he lowered himself to the canyon floor and walked five miles until he found help.

"I've never seen anybody that had this much desire and tenacity to stay with it and stay alive," said one of his rescuers.

Aron knew he was in trouble and faced his situation head-on. He hadn't expected a crisis, but when it came he dealt with it. Because of his determination and refusal to give up, Aron not only survived, but he grew strong through his ordeal. Aron says, "I had to make a decision to go forward, not knowing what was going to come."

When asked what was the most significant lesson he learned, Aron said, "We each have it within ourselves, through courage, faith and perseverance, to turn adversity into possibility."

Few of us will face hardship as traumatic as Aron's, yet adversity is certain to visit us all. Troubles and challenges are a part of life on planet earth. An old country pastor once said that there are only two types of people in the world—those who are wounded and those who are liars. I believe he had a point. We all face difficult, unfair, painful situations, and most leave their mark.

So the important issue is not whether we will be injured, but rather:

- Which wounds most need my attention?
- How are my wounds affecting me?
- Where am I on the path of healing?
- How can my wounds make me a stronger person?
- How can God use my wounds for good?

When we slow down and force ourselves to be honest, we often realize that all is not as it should be in our lives. Certain emotions such as anger, anxiety, fear, depression, insecurity, irritability, defensiveness, confusion, negativity, melancholy, and hopelessness are potential signals that somewhere deep in our hearts is a wound that is still tender.

Some of us know how to assess our wounds and what sort of attention each one needs, but many of us don't. So let's gain a little better understanding of the varieties of hurt.

NINE KINDS OF WOUNDS

While the categories of male hurts are numerous, here are some that I've found to be most common:

Physical wounds. Your body is what allows you to operate in this world. When it betrays you—through disease, injury, accident, genetics, or aging—it forces you to face life differently. These wounds are like shrapnel. They limit you and your potential, temporarily or permanently.

Bad choices. Sometimes we make selfish, stupid, or impulsive decisions that lead to painful consequences. We all have our regrets. If we could only go back and choose differently, most of us would do so in a moment. But here we stand in the midst of a mess, with no one to blame but ourselves. Which only makes the pain worse.

Verbal wounds. Words can be as painful as any physical wound, sometimes even more so. When grenades are hurled, intentionally or unintentionally, by those we respect or trust, the hurt can cut us to the core. Words of discouragement, rejection, or ridicule can easily squash us, stealing our confidence and our dreams.

Social wounds. We all want to be liked and respected. So when we are humiliated, excluded, or attacked by others, the resulting wound is real. Yet we frequently tell ourselves we shouldn't care. We try to act tough and ignore our wounds. But this does not ease the pain. Injurious treatment by people takes its toll on us, whether we wish to admit it or not.

Family wounds. Wounds from anyone can hurt. But if you feel rejected, disrespected, or injured by family members, it can be devastating. You expect support and caring from your parents, wife, and children. When parents turn against you, when your marriage falls apart, when children rebel, the pain can be intense. In some cases, you may feel as though your whole world is caving in.

Spiritual wounds. When we feel hurt by a church, a fellow believer, the clergy, or God Himself, the wound can lead to overwhelming spiritual loneliness and depression. We conclude that if God or His people wound us, He must be against us or not care about us. And who can stand against God? At this point, our wounds feel like a curse, with no remedy and no hope of healing.

Financial wounds. The ability to provide for one's family's basic needs is a part of being a man in our culture. Financial crisis and the need for financial help from others usually make a man feel as though he hasn't met one of his life's central obligations. A sense of failure haunts and burdens him. This can easily carry with it guilt, humiliation, and self-reproach.

Occupational wounds. An old saying declares that work makes the man. As guys, too often we wrap up our identity in our jobs. So the wound cuts deep if we're fired, laid off, unemployed, stuck in a dead-end job, or just don't like what we do. For the same reason, our sense of identity takes a hit if we feel harassed, ignored, minimized, abused, or powerless on the job.

Emotional wounds. Each of the above wounds carries with it an emotional component. Sometimes the original wound is buried so deep beneath the feelings that we can't even find it. We are only aware of a deep, overwhelming, anonymous ache and a cloud of emotions surrounding it.

These emotions confuse our thinking, blur our judgment, and too frequently block our awareness of God's caring presence with us.

Most wounds are some combination from among these nine types. No matter what the category of wounding, every hurt reminds us that we live in a broken world and cannot make it on our own. Wounds keep us from a positive, accurate sense of who we are and may lead us into a downward spiral pattern of low self-estimation.

The truth is, each one of us is a package containing great potential and great limitations. The book of Genesis teaches that humankind was made in the image of God and from the dust of the earth. Our Creator is well aware of our humble origins—and always takes them into account. David tells us that "he knows how we are formed, he remembers that we are dust" (Psalm 103:14, NIV).

Our spirit longs to soar, but our wounds tether us to the ground. They hold us back and force us to lean on the One who can truly heal all wounds. "Listen to my cry," says the psalmist. "For my life is full of troubles" (Psalm 88:2–3). We all have our troubles, and each one has the potential to create a wound.

Just the other day I was speaking to a handsome, confident CEO of a successful company about why his relationships fail and he feels so empty inside.

"Why don't you tell me about the greatest hurt in your life?" I asked.

"I don't have any hurts," he laughed. "After all, I make ten times more money than you. I can get anything I want."

"Tell me about your childhood."

"It was tough, but it taught me character," he responded glibly.

"What made it so tough?"

He then told me how his father had abandoned the family when he was four. His mother did the best she could as she went through five more husbands and a multitude of boyfriends.

"Were you close to any of them?"

"No," he said thoughtfully. "They were mostly jerks who didn't want to have anything to do with me. I was a stupid nuisance that was just in the way." He wiped something from his eye and demanded, "Why are you wasting my time with ancient history? Let's get down to business."

"I think we just did," I said. "As a kid you felt rejected at a crucial time when you needed security. That left a gaping hole in your heart. You stuck a bandage on the wound, but it hasn't yet healed."

"But how can that be?" He looked at me intently. "It's been thirty years!"

"Most memories fade over time," I explained, "but traumas, no matter how old, tend to stay raw unless treated."

Certain wounds touch the very core of who you are. Personality, situation, or age can increase a man's vulnerability. The intensity or duration of the injury, or the identity of the offender, can also make them more painful. For a variety of possible reasons, these soul-shaping wounds are more traumatic than other difficulties we may face.

Most memories are stored in our minds chronologically. As time passes, even if the facts and images remain vivid, the emotional intensity softens, and they have less impact on the here and now. Traumas, however, are stored topically. This means the pain does not fade with time. When we focus on this type of wound, whether the pain occurred long ago or yesterday, it packs the same intensity as when it first happened.

HOW IS YOUR WOUND IMPACTING YOU?

Facing your hurts head-on and recognizing how they might be affecting you is the first step toward healing. You may have become so accustomed to your wound that you're hardly even aware of it. Absence from awareness, however, doesn't mean nonexistence. That deep hurt you've covered up, denied, and run away from can still affect your life in many not-so-subtle ways.

Here is a diagnostic list of twenty common symptoms of emotional trauma. As you read through the list, be cautious of the tendency to rationalize, minimize, or explain away your symptoms. Try not to dismiss your responses to pain with statements like, "This is just the way life is," or "Everybody has their hurts," or "I could be doing a lot worse." Which of these show up in your life?

1. You are surprised by spontaneous emotions with no apparent cause.

2. You find yourself eating when you aren't hungry.

3. You are anxious about taking risks.

4. You have difficulty trusting people, even yourself.

5. At times you don't like yourself.

6. Feelings of guilt and shame can be overwhelming.

7. You struggle with periods of deep anger or depression.

8. The world doesn't feel like a safe place.

9. You wish you could live your life over again.

10. You feel like something is wrong with you.

11. You are easily startled.

12. You feel isolated and detached from others.

13. You do certain things to try to numb yourself to pain.

14. Your future doesn't seem very positive.

15. It's hard to let go of the past.

16. You're always expecting something bad to happen.

17. Life doesn't seem fair.

18. Nightmares, flashbacks, or emotional flooding can leave you upset for days.

19. Feeling safe and in control is very important to you.

20. It's hard for you to fully relax.

THERE IS ALWAYS HOPE

Wounds are a part of reality, and reality frequently serves up hurt and harshness in large portions. When I stood on the beach at that lowest point of my life, I cried out to God but heard no response. It was at that moment I turned to wise and godly counsel. Surely they could give me hope. They told me to pray more and read Scripture more and trust God more.

These are good things. Every one of them.

But they did nothing to ease my pain.

Instead, my friends' answers felt like salt and sand rubbed deeper into the wound. My "counselors" gave me formulas. But nobody *listened*. Nobody came alongside me. Nobody encouraged me. They gave their quick fixes and kept their distance. I shook my head and walked away, feeling alone and abandoned.

Coming out of this situation, I became determined never to leave a wounded man behind. I wanted to learn how to encourage those in pain and do what I could to pull them off their battlefields for first aid and healing. In Jeremiah's darkest hour he heard God say, "I will give you back your health and heal your wounds" (30:17). This is the promise we all yearn for when we feel most desperate and hopeless.

The twenty-two-year-old Charles Spurgeon was considered the most popular preacher of his day. By the time of his death, at fifty-seven, he was regarded by many as the greatest preacher of all time. Between these two dates, Charles experienced persecution, suffering, and discouragement. Someone once wrote, "There are few men that would not have succumbed to...the difficulties which had surrounded him." Yet he preached every chance he got, drawing large crowds. And he wrote nonstop throughout his career.

Charles believed that our wounds make us better people. He wrote, "Trials teach us what we are; they dig up the soil, and let us see what we are made of." He also wrote, "Many men owe the grandeur of their lives to tremendous difficulties." At thirty-three, his beloved wife became an invalid who could rarely leave her bed. Shortly after this, he suffered from a series of ailments that stole his good health and left him in severe chronic pain the rest of his life. Then came the darkness of depression, which left him "so low that I could weep by the hour like a child and yet I knew not what I wept for."

Regardless of his wounds, Charles marched forward. He refused to give up, he would not step down, and fading away was not an option. His philosophy was always strong and clear: "All that befalls us on our road to heaven is meant to fit us for our journey's end." After all, "The Lord gets his best soldiers out of the highlands of affliction."

FACE REALITY CHAPTER 2

GUYS HATE WOUNDS.

And we hate even more to admit we have wounds. We tighten our jaw, grit our teeth, and gut it out. We avoid doctors, dentists, and counselors unless our pain becomes unbearable. We know this is dumb, but we are guys, and denial runs bone-deep in us.

When I was about ten, I was out in the woods with my cousins picking berries. My Uncle A. J. came up to us and said, "Don't eat those; they're poisonous. They'll kill you."

My cousins threw their berries on the ground, but I had already eaten several handfuls of them. They were bitter, but they didn't taste that bad. I now faced a quandary: Do I tell my uncle that I've already eaten a bunch of berries so he can rush me to the hospital to get my stomach pumped, or do I just die? I wasn't sure how to tell Uncle A. J. And besides, I was afraid he would think less of me. So I decided to die. That night I organized my possessions, told my parents how much I loved them, and went to sleep, never expecting to wake. The next morning I was shocked to be alive. I thanked God for saving me and never told anybody this story. Until now.

The moral of this incident is that many guys would rather die than admit we have a problem. We would also rather die than face embarrassment or humiliation or loss of respect. Very early in our lives we learn that as men we have a certain code of conduct. Rarely does anyone talk about his code, but we are infused and surrounded by it, and our culture reinforces it in hundreds of subtle and not-so-subtle ways. These are the rules that we hold on to, even if we realize they may be irrational or unrealistic. Some of the rules are:

1. Men don't fail.

2. Men are always strong.

3. Men don't say or do dumb things.

4. Men must be in control.

5. Men don't cry.

6. Men take care of their own problems.

7. Men don't ask for help.

8. Men must be right.

9. Men protect themselves at all costs.

10. Men don't depend on anybody.

Being male and wounded is not a blend that our culture accepts as valid. Yet it is reality for all of us—a reality that a guy is never supposed to admit. Therefore, we are left isolated and lonely. Our hearts feel empty, and the pressures of our lifestyle kill us at a much faster rate than necessary. As Herb Goldberg writes in *The Hazards of Being Male,* "The male has paid a heavy price for his masculine 'privilege' and power. He is out of touch with his emotions and his body."

Nearly every day of the past twenty-five years, I've dealt with wounded people. From this experience I've observed that men hurt just as much as women. In fact, men frequently take loss, rejection, and failure harder than women. Men are more likely to cover up their wounds and hold their hurt in, while women find it easier to face their wounds and let their hurt out. Because of this, men tend to experience their hurt longer, and their wounds do not heal as completely. Men try to avoid their wounds through work and distractions. They don't feel as comfortable talking about their pain, because they often see it as a sign of failure or incompetence—a minimization of their manhood. Women view wounds as an expected part of their life experience. They speak openly with trusted friends about their challenges and seek advice from mentors or professionals; they see getting help as a healthy strategy for healing.

Men like to stick with what they are good at and avoid what they aren't good at. If we are good at golf or mechanics or geography, that's where we spend our free time. If we do something poorly, we will use any reason we can find to avoid it. Guys don't like failure of any kind, because it looks like weakness.

When anything that smacks of failure—suffering, crisis, wounding—enters our experience, we fight like wildcats to get away from it. Patrick Morley, in his book *The Man in the Mirror*, writes about five ways we resist the reality of suffering:

1. We plead: *I want something better.*

2. We compare: *I should have what they have.*

3. We pout: *I don't deserve this.*

4. We shout: *I hate this.*

5. We doubt: *I think God has abandoned me.*

These methods keep us from dealing with our wounds in a healthy way that brings healing.

Another way we avoid facing our wounds is through addictive behavior. We become so wrapped up in distractions that numb our focus or absorb our attention that we exempt ourselves from having to deal with the pain. In fact, at that point we may even be able to convince ourselves that the wound doesn't exist. We don't want to face reality, because all too often reality hurts.

Anything can serve as an avoidance strategy that keeps us from facing or resolving the wound at our core. Here are some types of potential avoidance addictions:

- Alcohol, tobacco, or drugs
- Work
- Thrill-seeking
- Sexuality or pornography
- Physical fitness
- Sports
- Television
- Collecting things (like cars or tools)
- Achievements or recognition
- Projects
- Hobbies
- Ministry

Some of these means of avoidance are not bad in themselves. But when obsession with them functions to screen you off from your inner reality, sooner or later they will create an even bigger problem.

HIDE AND TRY NOT TO SEEK

"Your dad has six months to live."

Sixteen-year-old Josh heard the words, but they didn't seem real. *The doctors are lying,* he rationalized. *They don't know what they're talking about. He doesn't look that sick.*

What do you do when you find out your dad has cancer? How do you deal with the fact that the man who has been your provider, your rock, your security won't be there? Josh couldn't grasp it. He moved into denial. He pretended that everything was still the way it had always been, and he prayed that nothing would ever change.

He couldn't talk about it.

He was afraid to even think about it.

When his father died exactly six months later, Josh was in shock. It couldn't be true. Since denial was no longer possible, Josh switched to a new strategy: avoidance. He drank heavily and jumped into a romance with all his heart. Alcohol and sex numbed the pain of his wound. It distracted him from reality for a time, but he knew it was just a diversion. When the anesthetizing effect of alcohol wore off and romance faded, Josh found himself face to face with his pain. It hurt so bad he thought he'd die.

Facing reality involves owning our wounds and admitting that we are not immune to pain. We must accept the simple fact that wounds happen and they can never be completely avoided. M. Scott Peck's classic, *The Road Less Traveled*, starts with these words:

Life is difficult. This is a great truth, one of the greatest truths. It is a great truth because once we truly see this truth, we transcend it. Once we truly know that life is difficult—once we truly understand it and accept it— then life is no longer difficult. Because once it is accepted, the fact that life is difficult no longer matters.

As men we can accept that life in general—"out there"—is difficult. But to admit that our personal life is difficult is a different matter. The idea of acknowledging our own wounds suggests an inability to deal with the challenges that face us. Men ought to be able to handle anything. Nothing should set us back or pull us down.

For many, wounds are hard to accept, but conceding to the emotions behind the wounds is even more arduous. Men are not supposed to struggle with emotions. We are brawn and brain. Emotions are messy. We know we have them, but they are not to be spoken of or shared with others. We guard them as our own private secret.

Following are ten emotions that guys hate to admit; we hide them carefully behind those wounds which we emphatically insist don't really exist:

Anxiety: I feel nervous and uneasy. I'm worried that something bad is going to happen. My stress is high and I'm not sure what to do.

Apathy: I have lost my motivation and I don't feel like doing a thing. Everything looks like it takes too much effort.

Confusion: I don't know what is going on. Nothing makes any sense. I can't seem to think clearly or grasp why this is happening.

Despondency: Life hasn't been fair. I feel depressed, discouraged, unhappy, and miserable. Nothing is going my way and it never will.

Helplessness: I can't handle this by myself. I am in over my head, and nothing I do seems to make things any better. I need help, but I hate to admit it.

Hopelessness: I'm frustrated. The present seems dark, and the future doesn't look any better. I don't think there's anything anybody can do.

Regret: I wish I had done things differently in the past. My choices and actions have made life difficult. If I could only live my life over again.

Paralysis: I'm frozen and unable to make any decision. All the choices before me have negative outcomes. Nothing I do seems to make things any better.

Uncertainty: I seem to question everything and everybody, especially myself. I don't know what to do or how to do it.

Urgency: Time is running out. I've got to do something to fix this as soon as possible. If things don't change quickly, something terrible will happen.

These are all common emotions that wounded warriors frequently feel. You can ignore, deny, or suppress them, but they won't go away. Avoidance might allow you to feel better for the moment, but the pressure will build, and sooner or later the emotion will burst out of your mental restraints, causing tenfold pain.

It's time to unashamedly speak the truth about our wounds. Augustine admitted in his *Confessions*: "I carried about me a cut and bleeding soul." King David cried out: "My heart is in anguish" (Psalm 55:4, NIV). To admit our wounds is:

- to be honest.
- to be real.
- to be courageous.
- to be humble.
- to be healthy.

In his book, *Will I Ever Be the Same?*, H. Norman Wright reminds us, "Crises are a normal part of life.... We can't avoid them, but we can handle them in such a way that they don't cripple or devastate us for the remainder of our lives." This is the challenge for us all.

Pete was a man's man. Nothing ever got him down. When his marriage failed, he scoffed, "You win some and you lose some." When he lost his job of ten years because of "corporate downsizing," he bragged that he'd finally found his freedom. Finally, when his mother passed away of cancer, Pete's tough facade crumbled. He cried like a baby, feeling vulnerable and abandoned. As we talked, Pete told me that his mother never told him she loved him and that he could not remember one time she'd hugged him. He admitted that the wall of control he built around himself was just a way to protect the ten-year-old little boy who'd cried himself to sleep each night. As Pete faced reality, he admitted his wounds.

And he became real.

CHAPTER 3
RUNNING FOR COVER

DOUG'S WOUNDS WENT DEEP.

Yet on the surface, they were nearly invisible to everybody except to those who knew him well. Doug had learned to hide his wounds, but what gave him away was his fear. He had learned early to trust no one, for everybody will sooner or later let you down. His father abandoned the family when Doug was eight. Two years later his mother married a rough, in-your-face, no-nonsense sort of guy. Doug's stepfather ridiculed him and called him all sorts of demeaning names. Doug tried to talk to his mother about this, but she simply told him to grow up and stop complaining.

At thirteen, Doug withdrew to his room and built thick emotional walls around his heart. He swore he'd never let anyone hurt him like this again. His fear of abandonment, rejection, and ridicule locked him deep within himself. When he married Sheila ten years later, he remained cautious and self-protective. Doug's fear of trust and letting his true self out almost destroyed his marriage. Yet Sheila was patient and wouldn't give up.

Doug saw the world as unsafe and every person he met as potentially hurtful. Danger was always just around the corner. Inside his heart was a thirteen-year-old boy, constantly on guard, anticipating the next attack. Yet on the outside he was cool and collected. He wouldn't let anybody know he was afraid. If asked about it, he'd laugh and change the subject. Feelings were uncomfortable for Doug, and when fear crept up on him, he would run for cover.

Feelings are often frightening and difficult to understand. To guys they seem messy and distracting. They slow us down, confuse us, and keep us from accomplishing things as smoothly as we'd wish. Yet feelings are a part of who we are, and fear is unavoidable in a broken world. We can run and hide and deny all we want, but our evasive action doesn't change reality. Avoiding fear only intensifies our pain, and avoiding pain only intensifies our fear. As a good friend of mine once said, "Pain feared is worse than pain endured." We must give ourselves permission to feel.

Wounds happen to all of us. Trauma strikes without warning. Because we live in a world filled with unpredictable and threatening situations, often beyond our control, we will never fully eliminate our fears. We are all afraid. As infants, we fear loud noises. As children, it's darkness and strangers that we dread. As teenagers, it's rejection and humiliation. As adults, it's failure and loss. As elders, it's change and death. Bruce is afraid of losing his job. Jeremy is afraid of losing his wife. Rob is afraid of crowds. James is afraid of the unknown.

And me? I'm afraid of heights. It might have begun when I was fourteen. That was the summer some buddies and I had a job thinning apples in the Columbia River Gorge. The Gorge is known as one of the best locations in the world for wind surfing. Every afternoon, about two o'clock, a hard wind would blow down the valley. This was great for a wind surfer, but if you were standing on the top step of a sixteen-foot ladder thinning apples, it was not a good thing. As I stretched high into the tree's upper reaches, my ladder would sometimes violently shake and then fall.

I was terrified. My heart beat violently, sweat broke out, and my head swirled. I would frantically grab a branch, hold on for dear life, and yell as loudly as I could for help. My buddies would come running and stand beneath me asking, "What are you doing up there?" "How long can you hold on?" and "If you were a real man, you'd just let go and fall." I'd yell and scream and threaten them as I slowly lost my grip. Then just before I fell to what I was sure would be my untimely death, the ladder was placed beneath my feet.

Now, years later, heights can still scare my socks off. But I refuse to let this limit me. I learned years ago that avoidance increases anxiety. So I climb tall ladders, conquer high-altitude rope courses, and take regular plane trips. None of these activities feel completely comfortable, but I won't let my anxiety limit me. Life is full of fears and the world is never fully safe. When a fear grips my heart and mind, I remember the powerful words of Paul Tournier: "The adventurous life is not one exempt from fear, but on the contrary, one that is lived in full knowledge of fears of all kinds, one in which we go forward in spite of our fears." Courage is not the absence of fear. It's honestly admitting our fears, embracing them, and working through them.

Because this world is broken and we are all wounded, fears will periodically grip us. No one is completely fearless. As guys we may fear that:

- something bad will happen.
- we will lose control.
- we will prove inadequate.
- the future will be horrible.
- the hurts of the past will revisit us.
- we will fail our loved ones.

There is no end to the fears that can potentially haunt us. E. Stanley Jones wrote, "Fear is the sand in the machinery of life." It can easily shut us down or tempt us to run for cover.

But it doesn't need to. Franklin Roosevelt was concerned with the ways that the Great Depression of the early 1930's had frightened the American people. Many had lost their homes, their savings, and their jobs. But worse than this, fear had frozen them. FDR knew that battles are frequently won or lost in our minds and attitudes. So he boldly declared, "We have nothing to fear but fear itself."

FACE YOUR FEARS

Are your fears limiting your life? Are anxieties undermining your peace of mind? Is worry making you miserable? Stop running. Stop hiding. Stop avoiding. Martin Luther wrote: "Courage faces fear and thereby masters it." To face fear robs it of its power.

The story is told of a young man who was being pursued by his fear. Everywhere he went, the fear was right behind him. He ran as fast as he could, but could not escape. Soon he was obsessed by his fear and it kept him from sleep. He was exhausted.

One day he went to an old grey-haired man who was known throughout the land for his wisdom. "How do I get rid of my fear?" asked the young man.

"Stop running away," said the old man.

"But I can't…"

"Sure you can," said the old man. "Stop running away. Turn around and run as fast as you can toward your fear."

The young man was skeptical. The old man's words seemed absurd. So he continued trying to outrun his fear. But one day he grew tired of constantly looking over his shoulder. The young man stopped in his tracks, turned around, and started running toward his fear. His heart beat fast and his anxiety grew. But surprisingly, his "irrational" action felt good.

The young man and his fear drew closer and closer. Then suddenly the fear stopped, turned around, and ran away from the young man. From that day forward he was never again afraid of his fear.

Admit your fears. List them clearly and completely. Search them out, hunt them down, and get to know them. Stare at them eyeball-to-eyeball and find out what makes them blink. One of the best ways for you to do this is to ask yourself a few key questions:

- What exactly are my fears?
- How long have I had them?
- Where did they come from?
- When and where are they worst?
- How do they affect me?
- Why do they hit me so hard?
- When have I managed them most effectively?
- What am I willing to do about them in the future?

Answering these questions honestly allows you to move forward. It brings uncomfortable feelings to the surface where the process of healing can begin. Facing your fears provides you with the extra courage and energy you need, in order to gain strength and build a more successful life.

STICK TO THE FACTS

Most of our fears never happen. This was a truth that my client George had forgotten. His face was pale and he was gasping for breath.

"Are you okay?" I asked him.

"I can't breathe. I think I'm going to die."

"You won't die," I assured him. "You are having a panic attack. Breathe deep. Drink a glass of water. Slow down."

Ten minutes later, George was relaxed and everything felt fine.

When fear clutches us, we have trouble thinking clearly. We panic and jump to negative conclusions. Anxiety can short-circuit the brain, drawing us into worst-case scenarios where confusion and hopelessness exaggerate our fears. Many of our worries come from a tendency to overestimate the likelihood of a frightening event, as well as our propensity to amplify its potential for harm. Our imagination runs wild and our anxiety escalates. Soon we feel out of control.

Look at the facts. Gather more information. Ask questions. And remember that speculation and extrapolation can get anyone into trouble. Don't let your mind turn small issues into big issues. Keeping perspective is crucial to controlling our fears. My grandmother used to ask, "What difference will this make in ten years?" Great question. Most of the issues we get all worked up about aren't worth the time or energy.

It's one thing to prepare for the future, but it's quite another to build a fortress of anxiety about it. Mark Twain wrote, "I am an old man and have known many troubles, but most of them never happened." Still, it's easy to fall into the "what if" game, where we start to guess at everything that might possibly go wrong. And the possibilities are infinite!

Jesus said, "Don't worry about tomorrow, for tomorrow will bring its own worries. Today's trouble is enough for today" (Matthew 6:34). Charles Schultz summarized this when he wrote, "Dread only one day at a time." The future is full of uncertainties. No one—except God—knows for sure what tomorrow will bring. So be responsible for today and trust Him with tomorrow.

LET GO OF YOUR WORRIES

Worry is the most useless and unproductive of all human activities. It doesn't improve anything. An old Swedish proverb says, "Worry often gives a small thing a big shadow." Worries inject your fears with high-octane booster. They keep your fears alive and give them permission to follow you wherever you go.

To combat worry, you must understand it. So here are eight truths about worry:

- *It feeds on itself.* The more you worry, the more you can usually find to worry about.

- *It paralyzes you* emotionally, mentally, socially, spiritually, and physically. It freezes you in your tracks.
- *It steals your joy* because it focuses on what can go wrong and how bad things could become.
- *It drains your energy.* It wears you out and exhausts you, hindering your ability to problem solve and to move beyond your emotions.
- *It robs you of peace.* How can you feel peaceful or serene when your mind is full of anxiety?
- *It hurts your health.* Chronic anxiety and worry have been linked to weakened immune systems, cardiovascular disease, and clinical depression, just to name a few of its physiological effects.
- *It undermines your confidence.* It highlights the negative and points out what you *can't* do to help yourself or those you love.
- *It squashes your dreams.* It fills your imagination with the worst, pushing all that is positive and good out of the picture.

Fear leads to worry and worry only makes your life more difficult. It entrenches your fears more deeply in your heart and mind.

Letting go of your worries involves four steps:

1. *Stop.* "Don't worry about anything" (Philippians 4:6). When worries come, literally say to yourself, "Stop." Then

consider what a waste of time worry is, for all the reasons I've listed above.

2. *Refocus.* "Fix your thoughts on what is true and honorable and right" (Philippians 4:8). By an act of will, move your thoughts from a negative focus to something positive.

3. *Release.* "Give all your worries and cares to God, for he cares about what happens to you" (I Peter 5:7). Let go of them and hand them all over to God. (More on this later.)

4. *Rest.* "Come to me, all of you who are weary and carry heavy burdens, and I will give you rest" (Matthew 11:28). When you've allowed God to take your worries off your back, you can begin to relax. He is the One who will give you genuine rest and refreshment.

BE PRODUCTIVE

Morrie Schwartz refused to allow his fears to make him wither and withdraw. At seventy-eight, Morrie was dying of ALS, and he knew he had no more than a few months left. He couldn't move his legs or feed himself or do most of the things we take for granted. His most fearful moments came when his chest locked up and he couldn't breathe.

"These were the horrifying times," he admitted. Fear and anxiety overtook him. But then he would step back, allow himself to feel the emotions, and say to himself, "All right, it's just fear. I don't have to let it control me. I see it for what it is… I don't want to leave this world in a state of fright."

Each day was a painful fight, but Morrie insisted on living each moment to its fullest. He refused to give in to either his condition or his fear. He filled his time with friends, with whom he laughed and cried and shared the lessons he'd learned about life. He also wrote letters, did three television specials, and helped shape a book, *Tuesdays with Morrie*, which became an international bestseller. Morrie refused to be passive; when it came to fear, he pursued a purposeful plan, even if that plan meant preparing for death. Morrie refused to run for cover.

Fear wants to stop you in your tracks. Yet as Robert Frost said, "The best way out is always through." When some friends suggested we go on a high-altitude ropes course, I didn't want to miss an opportunity to confront my fear.

But when I stood looking at the thirty-foot-long log suspended some twenty feet above the ground, I began to question my sanity. I breathed deep and said to myself, *You can do it.*

Another voice begged to differ. *No, you can't.*

Yes, you can, I insisted, *and you will. Even if it kills you.*

I had no handholds at my disposal. Nothing to help with balance. In my mind I made the following simple plan to walk upright across the log.

1. Take your time.

2. Don't look down.

3. Keep breathing.

4. Stop for a moment (if you need to).

5. Focus on one step at a time.

6. Refuse to give up.

It was the longest ten minutes of my life. But I made it across. I was terrified, but I did it.

Courage is a choice. It clears the way through our fear. Robert Anthony wrote, "Courage is simply the willingness to be afraid and act anyway."

Wounds require courage. As a wounded man, you need the courage to…

- face your wounds.
- feel your feelings.
- admit your pain.
- beat your fear.
- take a step forward.
- ask for help.
- pursue healing.
- tell your story.
- risk additional wounds.
- trust God.

Courage is intentional; it acts. If your circumstances afford you any freedom of choice, if any control rests in your hands, then act. And when you find yourself with no control over your situation, you can still take productive, intentional action—that is, you can decide to give it to God.

GIVE IT TO GOD

If God created all things and owns all things and is ultimately in control of all things, why not give your situation completely to Him? God knows all and can do all. He is our rock, our refuge, our shelter, our protector, our rescuer. Fear flees from Him.

As the children of Israel escaped the slavery of Egypt, they found themselves trapped. The Red Sea lay before them; the massive Egyptian army approached from behind. Trapped in the middle, the people began to panic. Yet Moses shouted above the crowd, "Don't be afraid. Just stand where you are and watch the LORD rescue you" (Exodus 14:13, TLB). And God came through in spectacular fashion. The lesson is clear: When we are smart, we let our fears drive us to God. This is what the great heroes of our faith—Abraham, Joseph, Moses, Joshua, Gideon, David, Daniel—did. And none of them regretted it.

This world can be a frightening place, and its battles can terrorize the bravest of souls. Friends and enemies can both wound you. God is the only constant, the only object worthy of consistent trust. Faith is the only lasting solution to fear and anxiety. Phil Callaway contrasts fear and faith in the following ways:

Fear imprisons; faith frees.
Fear troubles; faith triumphs.
Fear cowers; faith empowers.

Fear disheartens; faith encourages.

Fear darkens; faith brightens.

Fear cripples; faith heals.

A warrior is naïve or just plain foolish if he tries to live without faith. The apostle Paul insists that "in every battle you will need faith as your shield" (Ephesians 6:16). A soldier without a shield is vulnerable and easily crippled on the battlefield. We all need a solid shield for life's fight. Yet we also need a soft pillow, which allows us to rest and find new energy. Echoing this truth, Phillip Gulley writes, "Fear can keep us up all night long, but faith makes a fine pillow."

Faith is the enemy of fear; it's both the shield in one hand and the pillow in the other. So look up. Give all those fears, anxieties, and worries to the only One who can really handle them.

A COURAGEOUS ATTITUDE

At thirty, Michael received a wake-up call.

Nothing could have prepared Michael J. Fox for the diagnosis: Parkinson's disease. The neurologist filled in the details: "Young onset, progressive, degenerative, incurable, very rare." Michael was dazed and confused; he refused to accept the diagnosis. After all he was a young, healthy movie and television star. The G.Q. man of the year, no less. Yet underneath the surface "my life was in flames." He struggled with alcohol abuse, a failing marriage, anxiety, and incredible irresponsibility.

He wrote in his autobiography, *Lucky Man*, that "exasperation, frustration, and fear were my constant companions."

As Michael faced his fears, he began to deal with his inner demons. Reality was frightening, but he began to accept it. He found the courage to stop his drinking and acknowledge his disease. He recognized that a life of fear was not really a life.

Fear is an integral part of life, just like our wounds. It doesn't make us inferior or diminish our manhood. It's a necessary aspect of who we are and how we live. It's one of the many challenges we all must deal with on the road to growth and maturity. I like the words of Joshua Marine when he writes, "Challenges are what makes life interesting. Overcoming them makes life meaningful."

Running for cover eliminates you from life's race. To say the apostle Paul lived a rough life is putting it mildly. He was beaten, whipped, stoned, jailed, and shipwrecked. He traveled many weary miles, facing dangers in the cities, in the deserts, and on the open seas. He lived through weariness and pain and sleepless nights (see 2 Corinthians 11:23–27). Yet he persisted with a resilient attitude. He wrote, "We are pressed on every side by troubles, but we are not crushed and broken. We are perplexed, but we don't give up and quit. We are hunted down, but God never abandons us. We get knocked down, but we get up again and keep going" (2 Corinthians 4:8–9).

Now that's a courageous attitude.

"I WAS FURIOUS!"

Sam slammed his fist into the arm of his chair with such force that I wondered whether he'd broken something. "If I could get my hands on him, I'd kill him. How could he do this to me, to my family?"

Sam's business partner and best friend, Jose, embezzled Sam's life savings from the company that the two of them had created. The business was bankrupt, Sam's house was in foreclosure, and he was broke. "Jose stabbed me in the back and made a fool out of me. What sort of man am I when I can't even provide for my family?"

Anger. Resentment. Rage. These are normal reactions when we are wounded. Betrayal and loss have a way of violating our sense of justice. In fury we cry, "This isn't fair!"

Life is full of frustrations and disappointments, and it can easily tick us off. When we're feeling wronged, hanging onto anger and seeking vengeance might seem like a satisfying, practical solution. It isn't. But neither is denying or stuffing our anger.

Anger feels masculine!

It provides a sense of power and control in the midst of pain. It is especially useful when we feel out of control. Men struggle to express hurt and fear, but we know how to express anger. We get angry at friends, relatives, strangers, cars, the government, our kids, machines, stupidity, disappointments, and even God. We yell, scream, swear, kick, slam doors, hit, speed, drink, threaten, explode, shut down, and shake our fist.

Billy Graham wrote, "Anger breeds remorse in the heart, discord in the home, bitterness in the community and confusion in the state." Anger can be dangerous. If you are not careful it can intensify your wound, making your situation even more painful. A man's temper reveals the worst in him. Here are ten potential dangers of unmanaged anger:

1. It covers up your wounds.

2. It keeps you from dealing with the real issues.

3. It reinforces bad habits.

4. It pushes people away.

5. It hurts the people you love the most.

6. It makes you grumpy, irritable, negative, impatient, or unhappy.

7. It undermines your health.

8. It builds until it becomes resentment, bitterness, or depression.

9. It hinders God from using you.

10. It blocks you from healing and being all you can be.

Unless you have a strategy to deal with your anger, it will grow. As it builds, it turns ugly. Solomon said, "A fool gives full vent to anger" (Proverbs 29:11). David, Solomon's father, simply wrote, "Stop being angry" (Psalm 37:8, TLB). But that's a lot easier said than done.

ADMIT IT

If you are hurt or angry, be honest with yourself about it. Wounds can easily and quickly stir up anger. The process of healing must begin with honesty. Don't minimize the painful event or how you feel about it, but don't exaggerate it either. Whether you say you're getting mad or frustrated or bothered or irritated or ticked off or provoked or resentful or displeased or annoyed, those are all just different words for anger. Don't deny it, ignore it, or bury it. Feelings we suppress don't really die; they just go underground into hiding. Only to reemerge at some unexpected time in the future.

Anger can come out in a lot of dangerous ways. Here are a few:

The Violent Volcano: When you blow, everybody knows it. It's loud and throws debris everywhere.

The Lava Flow: A slow, seething anger that burns through anything it touches.

The Steam Plume: A lot of hot air that looks scary and can scald your skin.

The Poison Vent: Quiet and invisible, but deadly. It may look harmless, but it can kill you.

The Pressure Bulge: Something is building underground. You know it will blow, but you don't know how, where, or when.

You might go so far as to acknowledge your anger, but you must also understand it, or you won't progress toward resolution. Asking yourself questions helps you understand your emotions and keeps you from reacting thoughtlessly. Emotions can be incredibly powerful. If you allow them to translate immediately and instinctively into actions, you can get yourself into a lot of trouble. Thoughtful questions allow you to slow down so you can evaluate what's going on and make a conscious decision about what you want to do.

An individual's anger is very predictable once you figure out that person's pattern. Still, people surprise me with their lack of self-awareness. They tell me, "I can't control it," or "I don't know what happened," or "My anger just explodes before I even know it." These statements might seem true, but they aren't. You can always control your anger; you just have to think before you act.

Take time now, during a calmer moment, to assess your personal anger pattern. Simply ask yourself a few questions, and then try to remember your answers when rage next arises.

- What triggers my anger?
- When am I most likely to feel anger?
- How do I express my anger?
- What can I do to reduce my anger?

CHOOSE YOUR PERCEPTION

One day I was driving and a car full of college guys started tailgating me. I sped up, but they kept right on my bumper, so close that they almost rear-ended me. I got ticked at their recklessness, and things got worse. They honked their horn, shook their fists at me, and shouted unintelligible words. I accelerated—five, ten, fifteen miles above the speed limit. They stayed right with me, but now they moved alongside my car and tried to force me off the road.

At this point I decided to confront the obnoxious punks. I pulled over to the side of the road and jumped out of the car.

"Didn't you see us?" one of the guys said as he ran up to me. "We've been trying to get your attention for the past ten miles. Something is wrong with your car. It's smoking and we were afraid it was going to start on fire or something."

It's amazing how fast my perspective changed. The obnoxious punks suddenly became good Samaritans.

How you think and feel about something is frequently based on your perception. If you assume you have a justifiable reason to be angry, you will probably become angry. On the other hand, you have the capacity to choose a positive perspective. You can choose to let someone off the hook and give them a break. You can choose not to be angry. Anger is a choice.

Slow down and put your frustration in perspective. You don't have to assume the worst. Frame your situation in as positive a way as you can. Talk yourself through your anger. It's often your inner dialogue that fuels and escalates your anger. Why not use that inner dialogue to cool down your emotional temperature? You can do this by choosing not to major on blaming, belittling, or bemoaning those who trigger you.

If you want to calm down, you can do it. Anger does not have to escalate. Self-discipline means you control your emotions, rather than letting your emotions control you. You don't have to react instinctively.

Your own negative attitude might be a bigger contributor to your anger than anything anybody else has done. You can choose to be patient, gentle, understanding, and humble. Easy? Not always. But this is the path to maturity and success. Solomon writes, "It is better to be patient than powerful; it is better to have self-control than to conquer a city" (Proverbs 16:32).

So when your anger starts getting out of control, sit down, breath deep, and lower your voice. Proceed softly and slowly. It's hard to explode when you speak in a soft, restrained tone of voice. If you can't calm down, remove yourself from the situation. Sometimes the best response is to get away so you can get a grip on your emotions.

Another way to calm down is to work out your anger through physical activity. Exerting yourself can reduce built-up tension and help you refocus your mind and emotions, halting and reversing the downward spiral that wants to drag you deeper and deeper into anger. In many situations, the longer the distraction, the more your anger dissipates. Go for a drive, mow the lawn, play a game of golf, or take a long walk. Anything constructive to point yourself in a new direction.

WATCH YOUR WORDS AND ACTIONS

When you are angry, it's easy to say things you will later regret. The words pile up in your head, begging to come out. Yet, once they are out, you can never take them back. Words are fierce weapons. They cut and hurt and destroy. They can burn bridges that might never be fully repaired. But when we feel hurt, we want to hurt others. James had good reason for writing, "Be quick to listen, slow to speak, and slow to get angry" (James 1:19).

Indiscriminately speaking your mind can easily make a situation worse. When I'm angry, I've learned that the last thing I should do is open my mouth. My anger tends to sharpen my words and make them sound harsher than I ever intended them. Solomon warned that "harsh words stir up anger" (Proverbs 15:1). Words can stir up *your* anger and *the other's* anger. When two people are hostile toward each other and neither is watching his words, things can degenerate very quickly. Harsh words are those that accuse, attack, insult, belittle, or are edged with sarcasm. The world has enough anger; be careful about stirring up more. When you do, it's like stirring up a bees' nest. If you aren't careful, you will get stung. And the more you stir, the more stings you'll receive.

Words can be bad, but our actions can get us into even worse trouble. When we're angry, adrenaline rushes through our bodies searching for a way out, any way out. Hitting, grabbing, pushing, shoving, kicking, or throwing are all means of reducing our adrenaline, but they will almost always make the situation worse. Tom, a good-natured carpenter, recently told me that his anger scares him. He told me that before he learned to take his temper seriously, he'd fly into a rage, breaking things and instigating stupid fights. There is never a good excuse for expressing your anger physically toward another person—especially toward women or children—unless the person poses a significant physical threat.

Paul says, "Don't act thoughtlessly" (Ephesians 5:17). When we are angry, we don't tend to think clearly. Strong emotions usually cloud our thinking. So next time you feel anger rising, before you say or do anything, here are a few questions to consider:

- Is this situation really that important?
- Do they honestly mean what they just said?
- Why did they just do that?

- Is this a situation of simple immaturity or foolishness?
- Am I overreacting or taking this too personally?
- In what ways might I share partial responsibility for this?
- Will my response improve the situation or make it worse?
- What would be a positive way to handle this?

As you stop and think, you are more likely to keep your mouth shut. If you find that too difficult, then politely excuse yourself and leave the situation. Getting away can frequently help you clear your head and calm down.

LET GO OF IT

Unresolved anger is extremely dangerous. Anger left to fester becomes a deep emotional infection that only worsens with time. Resolve your anger as soon as possible. Paul insists, "Don't let the sun go down while you are still angry, for anger gives a mighty foothold to the Devil" (Ephesians 4:26–27).

Don't let anger accumulate. The sooner you handle your anger, the better. Anger rarely goes away by itself. You have to do something about it intentionally. If your anger persists or is out of control, talk to somebody about it. Find a safe, trustworthy person who can help give you perspective. The more you can talk through your anger, the better you can understand it and learn how to control it.

Carlos Santana, the Grammy-Award-winning musician, knew his unfaithfulness was wrong. He loved his wife, but that didn't stop him. When Deborah, his wife of five years, found out, she left him. Carlos was devastated. Yet as he sat alone and reflected on his life, he realized that he was running away from a deep anger that he had been holding onto from his childhood in Tijuana, Mexico. Beginning at age nine and continuing for two years, he had been molested by a friend's father.

Carlos finally faced his hurt and anger. He went to his wife and told her about his humiliating secret. "It was scary, but I had to share the information from a point of healing." Deborah accepted him back, and they have now been together for thirty-three years. His wife explained, "Nobody gets through life without their heart being hurt....We just worked it through."

The anger almost destroyed Carlos and his marriage. The molestation ate away at him, turned him bitter, filled him with hate, and caused him to act out. Carlos learned that holding onto your wounds and anger warps your thinking. Failure to forgive traps you in the past. "You want to kick his ass for robbing you of your innocence, but you have to let go." Carlos learned to let go, and now he is truly enjoying life.

Letting go of anger means refusing to allow it to control us. Anger often drives us to take things into our own hands to "set things straight." If anger feels good, revenge feels even better. Oh, the sweet joys of payback. We nourish our bent toward vengeance with self-talk like:

- *Let me show you how it feels.*
- *If you can give it, you'd better be able to take it.*
- *I can't let you get away with that.*
- *An eye for an eye.*
- *Nobody does this to me.*
- *Let me give him a taste of his own medicine.*
- *If I don't make this right, nobody will.*

Revenge often feels like the right and fair and manly thing to do. But revenge rarely resolves our anger; it tends to sustain and fuel it. As we rehearse fantasies of retribution, we review the injustice of our wounds over and over again. With each painful image, our dreams of retaliation grow crueler and the chance that we will act on our anger increases. Thoughts of being mistreated, cheated, deceived, and taken advantage of can trap us in feelings of anger, humiliation, and hate. Vengeful thinking keeps us chained to our pain.

But we don't have to live at its mercy.

The past is the past. What happened has happened. Letting go is not easy. It feels like you are letting people get away with wrongs for which they deserve to be punished. But revenge is a boomerang that always returns to hurt you. In fact, the harder you throw it, the harder it strikes back. So give away your right to revenge. Give it to God; His ability to exercise justice is so much more effective than yours or mine could ever be. "Do not repay anyone evil for evil.... Do not take revenge, my friends, but leave room for God's wrath, for it is written: 'It is mine to avenge; I will repay,' says the Lord.... Do not be overcome by evil, but overcome evil with good" (Romans 12:17, 19, 21, NIV).

Freedom comes as we let go. Healing comes as we refuse to rehearse the wrongs committed against us. Peace comes as we give God all our pain and our passion for revenge. Henry Nouwen, a Catholic priest and Harvard professor, wrote: "Jesus changes our history from a random series of sad incidents and accidents into a constant opportunity for a change of heart." Yet a change of heart doesn't usually come easily or instantaneously. It takes time and effort. It takes an active choice. And it is well worth whatever it takes.

So "get rid of all bitterness, rage, anger, harsh words, and slander, as well as all types of malicious behavior. Instead, be kind to each other, tenderhearted, forgiving one another, just as God through Christ has forgiven you" (Ephesians 4:31–32).

FORGIVE IT

Forgiveness and letting go of anger are one and the same. In fact, the New Testament word for *forgive* means literally to "send away." If we do not forgive, we sentence ourselves to a life imprisoned by pain. We freeze ourselves in the past, weigh ourselves down with heavy grudges, and allow grief to arrest our emotional progress. Unforgiveness is too expensive. We don't have the time and energy to waste on it.

Forgiveness involves giving up our right to make other people pay for the wrongs they have committed against us. It's a choice, a decision of the will. Keep in mind that the *deliberate act* of forgiveness almost always precedes the *feeling* of forgiveness. There is often a time lag between the two, not because forgiveness doesn't work, but because your emotional wounds still need time to heal.

Maybe you've carried your pain and anger so long that you don't even notice how heavy the burden has become. Some experts estimate that up to 80 percent of health problems can be traced back to one root cause—unforgiveness. Without even realizing it, past offenses may be undermining your health and killing you. Once you put forth the effort to forgive someone, it's amazing how reenergized and alive you feel.

At the same time, C. S. Lewis reminds us, "Everybody says forgiveness is a lovely idea, until they have someone to forgive." Sometimes we struggle to do what we know is right because:

- we aren't ready to forgive.
- we're afraid of being hurt again.
- we're still angry.
- we don't want to admit we're hurt.
- we think they don't deserve forgiveness.
- the offender's apology doesn't seem sincere.
- we want to hold our anger over their head.
- certain offenses seem too big to forgive.

Some wounds have gone so deep that it's virtually impossible to get beyond the strong emotions on our own. We just can't do it. We know God has forgiven us; we know God commands us to forgive; we know forgiveness is healthy for us. Yet we can't find the ability within us to let go. These are the times when we learn that the power to forgive comes from above. God will always empower us to do what He asks of us.

God instructs us to forgive—not for His sake, not for the sake of the one who wounded us, but for ours. It is the course of action He requires, because He knows that forgiveness is in our best interest, a critical key to our full recovery. When we make the intentional choice to forgive, we open the door for God to do a creative miracle in our heart. Forgiveness gives Him access to our wound. Then He heals, restores, and redeems what has been stolen from us. Painful memories may rise again in our minds, but forgiveness allows us...

- to send them away.
- not to dwell on them.
- to release the anger from them.
- to see the positive side of them.
- to strip them of their negative power.
- to place them in proper perspective.
- to learn from them.
- to have peace about them.
- to allow God to bring down justice.

Letting go of our anger is hard work. As we practice it, we discover more and more that forgiveness and healing are one. This is the hallmark of the Christian faith. As Chuck Colson says, "Nothing is more Christian than forgiveness."

BE ANGRY

Now, having said all that, here's another truth: Anger can be positive. Some 375 times, the Old Testament says God was angry. He became angry when He saw injustice, abuse, cruelty, selfishness, and stupidity. Jesus was angry when He turned over the tables in the temple and when He confronted the Pharisees about their hypocrisy. One day when Jesus was in a synagogue, His enemies tried to trap Him into a moral dilemma, tempting Him to "work" on the Sabbath by healing a man's deformed hand. Jesus "looked around at them angrily, because he was deeply disturbed by their hard hearts" (Mark 3:5). Jesus became angry when He saw people in desperate need who were unfairly treated. His anger drove Him to come alongside those who were wounded. His anger would not allow Him to be passive. It motivated Him to feed the poor, heal the sick, encourage the rejected, comfort the mourning, and raise the dead.

Anger, when properly channeled, can be a good thing. Paul said, "In your anger do not sin" (Ephesians 4:26, NIV). Anger directed at the right target, expressed by the right method and with the right motive, can be effective. George Washington,

Abraham Lincoln, Gandhi, and Martin Luther King were all angry at the injustices they saw in the world. They each took a stand and channeled their anger into positive action, each of them leaving this world a better place.

So be angry. But be careful if your anger...

- stems from selfish motives.
- crops up too frequently.
- goes out of control.
- is directed at the wrong target.
- lasts too long.
- leads to bitterness.
- damages others.

Anger has its place, but most of the time it is not healthy and makes situations worse.

DAMAGED FOR GOOD

Jack hugs everybody.

He is always smiling and encouraging, but life is not easy for him. Jack was a long-haul truck driver, and he loved the open road. When he was fifty-two, his right leg was crushed between two trucks. His leg had to be amputated, and his company switched him to a desk job. Then the company downsized and eliminated his position.

No leg.

No job.

No money.

Jack calls this his downtrodden period. On top of this, he couldn't get his mechanical leg to work right, so he'd frequently lose his balance and fall flat on his face. "I'd lie on the ground and I'd be so angry I'd wonder, *What's the use of getting up?*" During this time Jack told me he was angry at "anything and everything." If you said the wrong thing, he'd just want to punch you out.

Jack's anger only made his life worse. He knew that if he held onto it, it would destroy him. So Jack gave it to God. Now he says, "Things are hard, but I'm trusting my Lord." Jack smiles a lot now. He works as a chaplain for the elderly and the disabled. His own struggles have cultivated in him a special gentleness and compassion.

"What about the anger?" I asked Jack.

He smiled and gave me a big bear hug. "Everything is and was in God's plan, so what do I have to be angry about?"

CHAPTER 5

SHELL SHOCK

"IT WAS TOO PERFECT TO LAST."

That's what C. S. Lewis wrote of the remarkable love between himself and Joy Davidman. Never had he met a woman who was both his intellectual equal and such a source of happiness. In their relationship they quickly progressed from acquaintances to deep friends to genuine soul mates. Joy's son described their passion as "a great love that grew between them until it was an almost visible incandescence."

Then cancer took her. Lewis was left with an overwhelming grief that paralyzed him emotionally. His life became "torture" and was filled with "mad midnight moments." To survive the gaping wounds he wrote down his thoughts and emotions in four blank tablets, which were later published as *A Grief Observed.*

It's a wonder that anyone survives such pain. Lewis wrote, "There is a sort of invisible blanket between the world and me. I find it hard to take in what anybody says." He slipped into lethargy; all he wished to do was "mope and snarl." He felt lost in the darkness, as if he was trapped in a cellar or dungeon. He felt as though no one understood, especially if they said they understood. Even God seemed far away. "Where is God?" he wrote. "Go to him when your need is desperate, when all other hope is in vain, and what do you find? A door slammed in your face."

He felt lonely, empty, and scared. "Reality, looked at steadily, is unbearable." All wounds hurt. Grief screams and shouts and cries.

Healing takes time. After fifty-five pages, processing his pain, Lewis wrote that when he turned to God, his mind no longer met that locked door. The wounds did not immediately vanish, but at that moment he discovered a friend sitting beside him in the dark. And it wasn't just any friend; it was One who had suffered more than any of us.

Grief is inescapable and is no respecter of persons. Every loss holds a potential sorrow. The more significant and personal the loss, the deeper the grief. Sooner or later everyone will be bruised by grief. Loved ones die. Rejection tears us apart. Health fails. Jobs are lost. Dreams are shattered. Accidents happen. Everyone has his date with grief.

Losses leave their wounds. These wounds either make us stronger or break us, but they will never leave us the same. Grief tests us like no other experience.

We are surrounded by grief. Sam, at ten, is grieving the divorce of his parents. Eddie, at forty-seven, is grieving his mother's Alzheimer condition. Ben is twenty-nine and griev-ing his inability to find consistent work, together with his sub-sequent bankruptcy. Thirty-six-year-old Chad is grieving his preschool son's diagnosis of leukemia. Grief is like quicksand. It can suck you in, pull you under, and refuse to let you go.

A client named Don once asked me, "What's wrong with me? I'm feeling so sad, it's hard for me to feel good about life. Everything hurts."

"Don, your father passed away two weeks ago," I explained. "You had a great relationship. You are going to feel miserable. Accept it. This is normal."

Henry Wadsworth Longfellow wrote, "Every man has his secret sorrows, which the world knows not." No one is immune to grief. King David wrote, "I am worn out from sob-bing.... My vision is blurred by grief" (Psalm 6:6–7). Jeremiah cried, "My wound is desperate, and my grief is great" (Jeremiah 10:19). Even Jesus struggled with sorrow. When Lazarus died, He wept. And in the Garden of Gethsemane He said, "My soul is crushed with grief to the point of death" (Matthew 26:38).

Grief is confusing and full of contradictions. It is not logi-cal. Our sorrow is full of irrational, intense, unpredictable mix-tures of emotion. It's hard to understand from the outside. Nor is the view often much clearer for the one trapped within grief's darkness.

The pain of loss is confusing enough. But we compound the mental chaos by adding several common myths, such as:

1. Grief is a bad thing.

2. All people grieve in the same way.

3. You should not be angry about a loss.

4. You should keep busy and try to think only about pleasant things.

5. With time you will get over the loss.

6. You must be strong and try to keep your feelings under control.

7. It's best not to focus on the loss or talk about it.

8. After grief is resolved, it never comes up again.

9. Sorrow should be a private thing.

10. If you have a strong faith, the grief will not be as intense.

Grief loves to break the rules. It follows no neat, orderly, step-by-step progression. Grief does what it wants, taking you on a journey that is often both frightening and overwhelming. Everyone's grief experience is different. Your wounds are unique and personal to you. Your healing process will also be exclusively yours.

SHOCK

Grief confronts us with the unthinkable. We cling desperately to denial. *This can't be happening. This must be a bad dream. It can't be true.* We struggle with disbelief and confusion. We grow numb and light-headed and experience a variety of physical sensations.

Hollowness in the stomach.

Tightness in the chest.

Lump in the throat.

Ache in the heart.

The void is great. The hole feels unreal. The emptiness can consume every waking moment. Nothing seems the same. Questions surround you.

Nicholas Sparks, bestseller author of *The Notebook* and *A Walk to Remember*, describes his devastation. When he first heard that his son, Ryan, had a severe developmental disorder, the questions flooded him. *What exactly is wrong? How did this happen? What can I do to fix this?* These questions were difficult, but they drove Nicholas forward and helped him deal constructively with his grief.

Questions attempt to bring order to your pain. Yet many of your questions seem unanswerable. Assumptions you once held with utmost confidence now appear uncertain. Doubts are many. The whys are overwhelming. The answers feel trite and shallow and irritating, almost mocking.

Sorrow can be terrifying; it can make you feel like you're losing your mind. Yet questions, no matter how disturbing and unanswerable, push you forward. They force you to interact with your grief; they keep you from running away from it.

TEARS

"I am weary of my crying."

So wrote Theodore Roosevelt, in his early twenties, when his father died of cancer. He described his father as his "best and most intimate friend." This unexpected tragedy was a "hideous dream" which triggered a grief that seemed to emotionally paralyze the young man. He wrote, "Sometimes, when I fully realize my loss, I feel as if I should go mad."

Theodore survived this difficult time and within a few years reestablished his emotional equilibrium, his mother and his wife were now the two most important people in his life. Then tragedy struck again. His mother died suddenly, and within a few hours his twenty-two-year-old wife passed away. The women were in different rooms of the same house. Theodore moved back and forth, trying to comfort each. He wrote in his diary that on that day the light went out of his life.

Yet Theodore decided he would not allow this deep and crushing grief to destroy him. He fought back, his mind set on "spending himself in a worthy cause." He determined to conquer fear and grief, so that he might experience life to its fullest. He went on to become a writer, explorer, military hero, President of the United States, and winner of the Nobel Peace Prize.

Tears do not always come easily to men. At first we try to hide them, convinced that they indicate weakness or immaturity. But in time we discover that tears signify just the opposite. As he was dying, Morrie told Mitch in *Tuesdays with Morrie*,

"Someday I'm going to show you it's okay to cry." Not only are tears okay—they're healthy. Tears soften the heart. They display honesty, strength, perspective, and compassion. Charles Spurgeon said, "The salt of tears is healthy medicine."

When we love, we risk tears. When Sheldon Vanauken lost his wife, Davey, he wrote, "The tears came freely, and I did not attempt to restrain them when I was alone. Indeed, for over a year, there was no day I did not weep." Tears let out the pain in our heart and cleanse our soul. As Leigh Hunt writes, "If we do not weep outwardly, we are torn inwardly."

Douglas H. Greshem could not cry. He was son to Joy Davidman and stepson to C. S. Lewis, and he was fourteen when his mother died. When Lewis, who was also his beloved mentor, died three years later, the tears would still not come. With his pain trapped inside, his healing was stalled. Yet Douglas finally allowed himself to express his sorrow. "It took me almost thirty years to learn how to cry without feeling ashamed."

Tears are a good thing—maybe even a beautiful thing. Washington Irving wrote, "There is a sacredness to tears. They are not the marks of weakness, but of power. They speak more eloquently than ten thousand tongues. They are the messengers of overwhelming grief, of deep contrition, and of unspeakable love." Tears remind us that all is not smooth and easy. We can fight them or embrace them. Pain is built into the landscape of life. Sooner or later we will face tough terrain and rocky roads. Pain drives us into deep, dark places where only

God can teach us. Tears cry out for His help. Pouring out our pain, loneliness, and emptiness to God brings us closer to Him. We learn to trust and lean on Him. For if God can help us through the hardest times, He can help us through anything.

COMFORT

God never promised to protect you from grief. Yet when grief comes to your door, He will stand beside you as the pain drives you to your knees. Then, when you are ready, He will help you to your feet so the two of you can walk together again. God reminds us, "When you go through deep waters and great trouble, I will be with you. When you go through rivers of difficulty, you will not drown!" (Isaiah 43:2). God will see you through. As you open your heart and cry out to Him, He is there. Edgar Guest puts it simply: "When sorrow comes, as come it must, in God a man must put his trust."

God is fully aware of your sorrow and knows the way through your pain. Jesus has experienced it all. Isaiah describes our suffering Savior as "a man of sorrows, acquainted with the bitterest of grief" (Isaiah 53:3, TLB). He understands your every need and can ease your every care. He is our Strength. Our Shield. Our Refuge. Our Security. And in the midst of our grief He is our Comfort.

- "The LORD is close to the brokenhearted" (Psalm 34:18).

- "He heals the brokenhearted, binding up their wounds" (Psalm 147:3).
- "I will turn the darkness into light before them and make the rough places smooth" (Isaiah 42:16, NIV).
- "I will bind up the injured and strengthen the weak" (Ezekiel 34:16).
- "God bless those who mourn, for they will be comforted" (Matthew 5:4).

God is a God of comfort. He will weep with you. He has not rejected you and will never leave.

When James Means lost his beloved wife after twenty-eight years of marriage, he wrote, "When death rips apart your family, you discover a bitter new reality. I am learning about adversity, loneliness and the trauma of pain." This was a crushing time for James. It forced him to slow down and think seriously about his life and his priorities. It also forced him to rethink his faith. *Is God really good? Is He fair? Is He loving?* Though the waves of sadness swept over James again and again with a terrible power, he concluded, "God has never failed to provide grace."

Because God is loving and gracious, He is also comforting. Of course we would all like to avoid sorrow, but God can use grief to shape and strengthen us. We are being forged in a fire that will temper us for greater strength and flexibility. We are being reconstructed, restored, and renewed. God will walk us through the fire, directing our steps and calming our heart. Through the pain, we will learn lessons and discover truth.

Keri West gained much through her sorrow, but what she valued most was the deepening of her faith. She found that the following expressions of God's compassion enriched her life in ways she would never have thought possible.

- When tears are the only language you know, God hears.
- When darkness envelops your way, God sees.
- When pain forces you off course, God stabilizes.
- When loss wears you down, God comforts.
- When grief suspends your progress and saps your hope, God remains.

THE LINGERING

Sorrow frequently has a way of lingering. God's comfort does not always mean a quick and clean resolution. Sometimes grief can hang on for years; sometimes you never get over it.

Harold was telling me about his mother's death when a tear fell from his eye. "I miss her so much," he said.

"When did she pass away?" I asked.

"Sixty years ago this summer."

"That was so long ago," I said. "Does it still hurt?"

"Only when I think about it."

That's the way with grief. It leaves a hole that can never be fully filled. You may experience God's comfort, but the loss never ceases to be a loss. Something is missing, and as you reflect on it, your memory brings back the sorrow. The wound may heal, but the scar remains. And it will always remain. Still, that doesn't mean you can't move forward with a strength and confident faith that expects God's victory in every painful experience.

"Jack was my big brother and my hero," wrote Johnny Cash in his autobiography. Jack was killed in a table saw accident when Johnny was twelve. "It was awful at the time and it's still a big cold, sad place in my heart and soul. There's no way around grief and loss: you can dodge all you want, but sooner or later you just have to go into it, through it, and, hopefully, come out the other side. The world you find there will never be the same as the world you left."

For many years Johnny tried to bury his terrible grief with frantic activity, alcohol, and drugs. Nothing took away the staggering loneliness. At thirty-five he'd had enough. He went alone into Nickajack Cave on the Tennessee River, intending to die. Instead he found an amazing sense of peace and clarity. Deep in the cave, Johnny discovered that God was with him, even in his darkest hour.

For the rest of his life, Johnny tried to live his faith. He described his life as "an incredible journey of trauma, oblivion and pain." Yet he also saw each day as inspiring, rich, and astonishing. God was his counselor and his Rock of Ages. Johnny sang honestly about his deep faith right up to the end of life, but he also sang fearlessly about the intensity of his wounds. Perhaps his battle is summed up in the title of his last hit song: "Hurt."

One thing you could always say about Johnny Cash is that he never let the hurt shut him down.

"I HOPE NOBODY EVER FINDS OUT."

"What are you afraid of?" I asked.

"They'd hate me," Allen said with a sad resignation. "They'd reject me. I've lost their respect. I've lost my reputation and credibility. I have nothing left. I'm the biggest loser of all time."

His pain and discomfort permeated the room. I wanted to encourage him, but all I could think to say was "But what if they forgave you?"

"But what if they *didn't*?" he shot back.

"What if you forgave yourself?"

"I don't know if I can." He grew quiet and reflective. "It just feels too big. I wish I could go back and do everything over again, but it's just too late."

I've had this conversation hundreds of times with hundreds of men about hundreds of wounds. Wounds like sexual addiction or rejection; dropping out of school or a nasty divorce; a best friend's suicide or unemployment with no idea how to pay the bills. I wish all the Allens of the world knew at least one thing: As long as you're alive, it's never too late.

We all have sins and secrets and embarrassments that haunt us. These are wounds we try to hide behind new cars, tough talk, bright smiles, hard work, and good deeds—anything to avoid being exposed.

Our wounds make us hypersensitive to guilt and shame. Most of us cover our pain. We don't want people to see our brokenness or failures. We all want to be loved and accepted. We all dream of being healthy.

One of the stories about Jesus that is, to me, most touching relates the time He encountered an unnamed woman caught in guilt and shame. (I've often wondered what happened to the man who was with her. Did they let him go or did he run away? Surely he was no less culpable than she. He too should have been brought before the crowd, for this should have been his story as much as hers.)

It was early in the morning, before most people had headed off to work. Over the last few days, Jesus had been teaching about living water, saying, "If you are thirsty, come to Me." A crowd had gathered to hear more, their spirits dry, thirsty for hope.

Suddenly there was a disturbance. Jesus heard shouting and struggling. A panicked, half-dressed woman was dragged into view, down the cobblestone streets, by strong men with stern faces. They pushed and dragged her until she collapsed in a heap before the curious crowd. She trembled and covered her tear-stained face. Her hair was uncombed. Her feet were bleeding. Her dress was torn. She pulled it tighter around her shoulders to hide her nakedness. But she could not hide her guilt and shame.

One of the men in authority shouted out the accusation: "This woman was caught in the very act of adultery."

Caught: "We got you."

In the very act: "There's no getting out of this one!"

Adultery: "How dare you? What were you thinking?"

Men gathered stones—sizable, with sharp angles. Clutching them firmly in impatient fists, they waited for the signal. They knew what to do. Throwing stones came easy for them.

Jesus, however, didn't pick up His stone. Inexplicably, He bent down and began writing in the dust with His finger. Nobody knows for sure what He wrote. But those who encircled the wounded woman knew.

Some think He wrote something like "If you forgive others, you will be forgiven" (Luke 6:37). Others think He wrote in front of each man a personal example of their secret guilt or shame. *Laziness, pride, greed, abuse, dishonesty, addiction, hypocrisy.* But whatever He wrote, it had its impact. Finally looking up, He said, "Let those who have never sinned throw the first stones."

Faces fell.

Hands loosened their grip.

Rocks dropped.

Sandaled feet left one by one.

All was silent.

In a gentle voice Jesus asked, "Where are your accusers? Didn't even one of them condemn you?"

She looked into those dark eyes of compassion and mercy. "No, Lord."

"Neither do I. Go and sin no more."

She stood slowly to her feet, awash in a mixture of relief and amazement. Her guilt had been forgiven, her shame washed clean, her wounds healed. She had been set free. Now came her greatest challenge: She must live like it (see John 8:1–11).

We are all like this woman in some way. Maybe our guilt and shame is still private. We know our failures and we fear what might happen if they are discovered. Or maybe we've already been caught. We feel the panic and vulnerability of exposure. We see the crowd encircle us, clutching their sharp stones. A few of us have even felt the sting of those stones as friends and family and even strangers have let them fly.

Or maybe we've seen God's grace and heard "You are forgiven." Some of us have experienced the tender compassion and warm encouragement of others. We have experienced the freedom that another wounded woman discovered when she fell at Jesus' feet "and told him what she had done." Jesus reached out to her. "Go in peace. You have been healed" (Mark 5:33–34). God's healing is the hope of all who have known the pain of any wound.

We have to stay on guard against spiritual infection. We must keep our wounds from festering into guilt and shame. These two intense emotions are closely related; sometimes they overlap. Yet they are distinctly different. Separate or combined, they form a powerful acid that can burn right through our peace and contentment. They can create great pain, derailing or destroying our plans and dreams.

But even acid has a purpose. Sometimes it's needed to eat through harmful attitudes and hard, unyielding hearts.

Our wounds can trigger guilt. That guilt, if not dealt with, can become shame. *Guilt* tells us that we've thought, said, or done something wrong. As a result, we believe that we deserve some sort of punishment. *Shame* tells us that we're just plain bad people.

Guilt is all about what we've done. Shame is all about who we think we are.

Fearing rejection or punishment, we withdraw, hoping things won't get any worse. Yet that very withdrawal traps us in our guilt and shame.

GUILT

We are *all* guilty. Let's get that out of the way right off the top. The Bible tells us that "all have sinned; all fall short of God's glorious standard" (Romans 3:23). Each one of us has thought, said, or done things that we have later regretted.

A seven-year-old girl once told her parents that she had to see Dr. Steve. They asked her why. All she would say was

"Something is wrong, but I can only tell Dr. Steve." Every day for two weeks she persisted. "I have to see Dr. Steve."

Finally the parents brought her to my office and the girl poured out her concerns. "My brain is broken," she told me with deep sobriety. "You know that thing in your head that keeps your thoughts from coming out your mouth? Well, it doesn't work for me. Whenever I think something bad, I just say it. Then I feel so bad because I don't want to hurt people."

Maybe we all have broken brains.

When my son, Dusty, was nine, I asked him if he ever lied. Without hesitation he looked me in the eye and said, "Yes, because 'All have sinned and fallen short of the glory of God.'" Then he thought for a minute and said, "Dad, do you know why that's such a good verse?" I shook my head. "It's because you can use it whenever you're in trouble." Then he added, "And for me that's almost every day."

Guilt is a part of being human. It's a recognition of our brokenness and weakness. It's a reminder that we are all wounded.

Guilt is a good thing. Like a light on your car's instrument panel warning you that something is amiss. (It also warns us to consult our Manufacturer!) It tells us when we have done something hurtful to others, ourselves, or God. It's a signal that we have broken our value system and need to change our behavior. Guilt comes from a healthy conscience. We *should* feel guilty if we lie or cheat or steal.

Kevin was handsome and articulate, but something about him left me deeply troubled: Kevin felt no guilt. None at all. He told me he loved his wife and that she was a good woman, but he was sleeping with her best friend. This had been going on for about two years, and he had created an elaborate web of lies to protect him from discovery. I was concerned about the affair, but I was more concerned with his lack of guilt and his twisted justifications.

"Sometimes things just happen."

"Guys will be guys."

"I couldn't help myself."

"She's better off not knowing."

"It's not like I'm hurting anybody."

"It's not my fault that she wouldn't understand."

"Some guys just can't be faithful to only one woman."

Kevin frightens me.

Think about it. Without guilt, he is capable of *anything*. There is nothing to stop him—no speed bumps to slow him down, no guardrails to keep him on the road. He can careen out of control and not even understand the danger. Or care.

Neither extreme is healthy. Kevin is an example of no guilt. But too much guilt can also take you down a dangerous path. I know men who feel guilty for everything from suffering physical abuse as a child to not making enough money.

We live in a world of "shoulds," and if we do not live up to our particular list of "shoulds," we frequently feel guilty. Yet the real question is: Are those "shoulds" of ours realistic or healthy or even achievable?

Should comes from the Anglo-Saxon word for *scold*. Too often we scold ourselves for not being perfect or not being able to make those around us happy. But nobody's perfect, so it's time to stop beating ourselves up. Here are a few common "shoulds":

- I should never make mistakes.
- I should never forget.
- I should always have a great attitude.
- I should know the best solution to every problem.
- I should never be angry or frustrated, or lose my temper.
- I should never hurt anybody.
- I should always be prepared for anything.
- I should never get sick or exhausted.
- I should never let anyone down.
- I should be strong.
- I should never let my feelings control me.
- I should always be perfect.

Healthy guilt keeps us in touch with reality. It points out spiritual dangers that are destructive to ourselves and those around us. In contrast, toxic guilt causes us to become fixated on our wounds. We scratch them, pick off their scabs, poke and squeeze them, and we don't let them heal. Toxic guilt makes a wound worse. Healthy guilt pushes us toward healing.

Corrie Ten Boom once wrote, "The purpose of being guilty is to bring us to Jesus. Once we are there, then its purpose is over." Healthy guilt seeks forgiveness and freedom. It yearns for a fresh start—not through denial or minimization, but through repentance and repair.

King David wrote, "My guilt overwhelms me…. My wounds fester…. I am deeply sorry for what I have done" (Psalm 38:4–5, 18). But he refused to let these things turn him into a bitter man. He cried out, "Come quickly to help me, O Lord my savior" (v. 22).

Turn your back on toxic guilt. And turn your healthy guilt over to God.

SHAME

Unresolved guilt frequently ends up as shame.

Brock was twenty-one when his wife left him. It was only two months after a large, elegant church wedding. She gave no reason; she just left and filed for divorce. Brock believed he must have done something wrong. After all, a nice Christian woman wouldn't walk out if he had been a good husband.

Several years later he moved to another community and married again. No one there knew his secret except his new wife. That is until an old friend came to visit and casually asked about his previous wife at a dinner party. People asked questions. Brock tried to change the topic, but it was too late. His face flushed and his throat constricted. He gruffly told them they needed to keep their noses out of other people's business. The room went silent. In the awkwardness that followed, Brock excused himself and did not return. After the party he shook his head and told his wife that he could never face his friends again.

Shame keeps its head down. It believes that if others see our wounds they will have nothing to do with us. Shame tells us that our wounds make us totally worthless and unacceptable. Sandra Wilson writes, "Shame is a strong sense of being uniquely and hopelessly different and less than other human beings." It says that if we are flawed, scarred, or limited, then there is nothing that can be done about us. It relegates us to the garbage heap. We internalize messages like "You're not good" or "You're not good enough." Shame begets shame. Fortunately, God has an answer for shame.

SHAME'S TALK	GOD'S ANSWER
I am damaged.	I will heal you.
I am dirty.	I will wash you whiter than snow.
I am incompetent.	I will teach you all you need to know.
I am stupid.	I will fill you with wisdom.
I am unwanted.	I made you.
I am weak.	In your weakness I am made strong.
I am hopeless.	I will give you hope.
I am unlovable.	I sent My Son to die for you.

| I am nothing. | You are My child. |
| I am worthless. | You are precious. |

Shame often magnifies and exaggerates our wounds. Under the influence of shame, specific and isolated wounds balloon out until we believe ourselves to be one big walking wound. Shame insists that our wounds now define every aspect of our identity. We can be nothing more than our wounds, and when people see us, we're convinced that is all they see.

This is paranoid thinking. If we deflate shame to its real size, stripping it of all exaggeration, we are left with a genuine core of five basic truths toward which shame points us. Shame is...

- a symptom indicating that something is wrong.
- a recognition of our limitations.
- a reminder that we are flawed.
- a defense against pride.
- a chance to better understand our wounds.

Readjusting our perspective by means of these truth-based lines of thinking allows our shame to become redemptive, rather than destructive. God's grace is ultimately the best cure for debilitating shame, for it takes away the two things that give shame its power—rejection and abandonment. God's grace wraps us in unconditional love and acceptance.

SO WHAT DO WE DO NOW?

No matter how painful something is, we must face it. Ignoring a wound does not make it go away. Robert C. Larson wrote, "Unfriendly ghosts from your past may never disappear entirely. They can return to haunt you at a moment's notice. The key is to keep meeting these apparitions head-on." Stare straight into the dark eyes of your wounds—remembering the situations, experiencing the feelings, dealing directly with the guilt and shame.

In *Healing of Memories,* David Seamonds writes, "The harder we try to keep bad memories out of conscious recall, the more powerful they become. Since they are not allowed to enter through the door of our minds directly, they come into our personalities (body, mind and spirit) in disguised and destructive ways."

If we hide from our wounds, rather than facing them boldly and directly, we may force them to resurface in even worse forms—namely, guilt and shame. But as we face our wounds, we can turn them into teachers, channeling guilt and shame toward their constructive role, so that they pull us out of the shadows rather than pushing us into them.

Grace and forgiveness are the cures to our deepest guilt. The first step toward health is to stop beating ourselves up for the past and to start forgiving ourselves. For what we did, and sometimes also for what we didn't do. Sometimes we need to forgive ourselves for letting false guilt torture and paralyze us.

If we are truly guilty, here are the steps along the path
of healing:

- *Repentance*: Admit to ourselves and those
  impacted that what we have thought, said, or
  done was wrong.
- *Remorse*: Feel genuine, heartfelt sorrow for the
  ways we have hurt God, others, and ourselves.
- *Restitution*: Do what we can to undo the wrong.
  Where the harm is irreparable, restitution might
  serve as an important symbol—something sacrifi-
  cial and related to the wrong to show that we take
  our sin seriously.
- *Repair*: Go to those we have wronged, seeking
  forgiveness, and then make specific changes that
  will help protect us from repeating our wrong.

Jesus said to the paralyzed man, "Take heart, son! Your
sins are forgiven" (Matthew 9:2). The Lord was giving the man
freedom. In that very moment.

If you've given God your sin and its guilt, you can let go. It's
God's. You're free.

Right now.

Forgiveness for ourselves allows us to let go of the past
and envision a new tomorrow.

Forgiveness toward others helps erase our shame. In
every wound there are people to forgive:

- People who wounded us or those we love.
- People who didn't protect us.
- People who deepened our wounds.
- People who didn't or wouldn't understand.
- People who lied.
- People who damaged our reputation.
- People who judged us.
- People who kicked us when we were down.

Forgiving others helps us detach from our guilt and shame. It lifts us above our wounds. Sure, some of these people don't deserve our forgiveness, but that's not the issue. If we refuse to forgive, we become trapped in vengeance or victimization. Forgiveness sets us free, and freedom allows us to use our pain to better ourselves and those around us.

As we forgive ourselves and others, we can freely embrace the forgiveness of God. David cries out, "O Lord, you are so good, so ready to forgive" (Psalm 86:5). All we need to do is ask with a sincere heart. God is willing to wash away our guilt and shame. The scars that remain are covered with His never-ending grace and touched with divine meaning. As the playwright Eugene O'Neil once wrote, "Man is born broken. He lives by mending. Grace is the glue."

CHAPTER 7
BATTLE PLANS

"YOU'RE LUCKY TO BE ALIVE" said the nurse in a soft voice.

"Why...why can't I feel anything?" asked the eighteen-year-old star athlete.

The nurse gently picked up his hand and touched his numb fingers. "You can't feel anything, Ron, because your body is paralyzed."

A surfing accident on Huntington Beach, California, left Ron Heagy a quadriplegic. One moment he was an energetic surfer with a full football scholarship to Oregon State University, and the next moment he was a helpless, broken child pleading with God not to die.

Some twenty-five years have passed since Ron's accident, but he has refused to give up. Ron speaks across the country, determined to make a difference, touch lives with his story, and give hope to hurting hearts. He insists that "nothing is wasted in God's plan. Everything works together for good."

Ron is one of the most positive people I've met. His wounds hurt, but his attitude soars. He says, "My ministry is about changed attitudes and changed lives." His is a story of

triumph over tragedy, of the power of joy. The title of his autobiography tells it all: *Life Is an Attitude*.

Wounds breed negativity, and negativity can become
more damaging than the wounds themselves. As Dale
Galloway says, "In the final analysis, it is your own attitude
that will make or break you, not what has happened to you."

Your attitude has incredible power. A positive attitude
strengthens your faith, deepens your peace, adds to your joy,
and improves your general health.

But when we're struggling with severe pain, any mention
of "positive attitude" seems forced and shallow, miles and
miles distant from our real, hurting world.

Maybe sometimes it is. But remaining negative is a dangerous business. Negativity is a whirlpool that can easily pull you
into its vortex and drown you in its darkness. Over the years I
have discovered the following four basic facts about negativity:

- *Negativity comes naturally*. We don't have to work
  at it! It's a reflex reaction to pain. The more exten-
  sive our wounds, the stronger and more long-
  lasting our negative mindset tends to be.
  Becoming positive takes an intentional, determined effort. In fact, it takes the power of God.
- *Negativity makes us feel worse*. Negative feelings may
  come easily, but they're poison to us. They intensify our
  pain and can trap us in the dark hole of depression.

- *Negativity pushes people away*. Most people steer clear of those who are consistently downbeat, negative, or cynical. This leaves us isolated and lonely. It causes us to feel even more worthless. Sadly, it distances us from the people we need the most.
- *Negativity keeps us from healing*. When we think positively, we search for help and focus on hope. But negativity keeps us focused on our wounds. It exaggerates the pain.

Our focal point determines how we think and how we feel. In the midst of the most painful period in his life, James Means wrote in *Courage in Crisis*, "The very fire that blackens my horizons warms my soul. The darkness that oppresses my mind sharpens my vision. The flood that overwhelms my heart quenches my thirst. The thorns that penetrate my flesh strengthen my spirit. The grave that buries my desires deepens my devotion." Finding the positive in the midst of the firefight gives us hope. It forges our character. Over time our thoughts and feelings will shape our identity and our future outlook.

To be positive we must be intentional. We must put our battle plans in order. Only a fool would enter a battle without a strategy. Successful soldiers know that battles are frequently lost or won in the mind. A winning, positive plan can turn the most difficult situation around. We can't control our past wounds or our current circumstances or the people around us.

But we can control our attitude. Attitude is everything. That's what Ron Heagy learned. Some people consider this the single most important factor in their life. Patricia Neal writes that "a strong positive mental attitude will create more miracles than any wonder drugs."

Some people are born optimistic. They find a silver lining in every cloud and see the glass half full. In keeping with the Ronald Reagan joke of old, they'll dig through a roomful of manure believing "there must be a pony in here someplace." They bounce back from difficulties and manage a sunny disposition on the gloomiest of days.

Then there are those who always have a dark cloud hanging over them. They have a hard time looking at the bright side of things. Whether positive perspective comes naturally or not, anyone can learn or develop the skill of optimism. Let me offer a general set of battle plans to get us started.

LET GO OF THE HURT

The healthy man always refuses to let his past pain destroy today's good. An ancient Japanese proverb says, "Let the past drift away with the water." Leave the past to the past. What has happened may have been tragic, but to let it mar the future is even more tragic. The prophet Isaiah says to "forget the former things; do not dwell on the past" (Isaiah 43:18, NIV).

Ken was abandoned by his mother. By the time he was fourteen, he had been in eight different foster homes and twelve different schools. When he was fifteen he ran away and lived on the streets for a year. Angry, depressed, and hopeless, he realized one day that he had allowed himself to become a victim—and that made him even angrier.

"I've seen too many victims," he told me, "and they are pathetic. I refuse to be a victim." Now at age twenty-two, Ken is working with the high school group at his church, and he's enrolled at the local community college. When I asked his secret for overcoming the anger and depression, he said, "Realize that you can't change what happened, but you don't have to be a victim of it."

The more we focus on the wounds of the past, the more we are victimized by them. Victims fall into the following traps.

- They are overwhelmed by the negative.
- They get stuck in the negative.
- They think of themselves as negative.
- They see the future as negative.
- They believe there's no way out of the negative.

To escape a victim's attitude, we must squelch all the negative self-talk about the past.

TELL YOURSELF THE TRUTH

We are constantly talking to ourselves. This self-talk shapes our perceptions and emotions. To become positive, we must stop our negative self-talk. The apostle Paul wrote, "Let everything you say be good and helpful" (Ephesians 4:29). This can just as easily relate to what we say to ourselves, as to what we say to others.

Words have power. Our words matter. *Even the words we speak to and about ourselves in the silence of our thoughts.* Such words will either build us up or tear us down. Negative self-talk looks at our wounds and says things like:

- God is punishing me.
- I deserve this.
- Life is unfair.
- I hate myself.
- Nothing ever changes.
- I am trapped.
- There is no hope.

Negative statements make us feel more miserable. They reinforce the victim mentality and suck us deeper into the quicksand of dark thinking and defeatist attitudes. They foster self-pity and paint a distorted picture of reality. They become self-fulfilling prophecies, so that what might have turned out better, gets worse.

Positive self-talk is like a safety line that can pull us out of despair. William James wrote that "we can alter our lives by altering our attitudes of mind." We change our attitudes by making positive and true statements to ourselves. In this way we follow the counsel of the apostle Paul, who wrote, "Let God transform you into a new person by changing the way you think" (Romans 12:2).

We can transform our thinking by renewing and revising our self-talk. That means repeating phrases like:

- God loves me.
- With God all things are possible.
- God wants the best for me.
- God will strengthen me.
- This world is temporary.
- I am never trapped.
- I can be content, regardless of my circumstances.

Positive self-talk can change our attitude, and with a changed attitude everything looks different.

HOLD ONTO THE LESSON

Our wounds teach us powerful lessons. As Benjamin Franklin said, "The things which hurt, instruct." Hurts and difficulties are possibly the very best experiences we can have. And though we often resent them and see them as negatives, they are truly treasures. Harriet Beecher Stowe, author of *Uncle Tom's Cabin,* wrote, "I long to put the experience of fifty years at once into your young lives, to give you at once the key to that treasure chamber every gem of which has cost me tears and struggles and prayers, but you must work for these inward treasures yourself."

Wounds have lessons to teach, and it's sad when we endure all of the pain but miss the valuable truth we might have drawn from our suffering. These lessons aren't easy—not by any means—yet even so, they are precious. Like the twists and turns that give the grain in wood character, so our wounds give us a depth and richness like nothing else can.

Karen Blixon had three loves in her life. Yet each left deep wounds. Her father committed suicide when she was ten. Her husband was continuously unfaithful and gave her syphilis, which had no treatment at the time. After eleven years in an unhappy marriage, they divorced. Then she fell in love with a man who was gay. For thirteen years he was her best friend, yet unable to return her love. When she was forty-six, he was killed in an airplane crash.

In spite of these tragedies, Karen kept a positive attitude. She wrote many books under her pen name, Isak Dinesen—books such as *Out of Africa* and *Winter Tales*. In reflection on her life she wrote, "I think these difficult times have helped me to understand better than before how infinitely rich and beautiful life is in every way."

PURSUE OPTIMISM

Jesus said that if we seek, we will find. If we ask, we will receive. If we knock, the door will open (see Matthew 7:8).

Jesus' brother James wrote that we don't have because we don't ask (see James 4:2).

Many times we don't experience health and healing because we don't intentionally pursue it. We wait for it to come to us and then grow impatient and ticked-off when it doesn't arrive in a timely manner.

Actively seek what is good and positive.

Chase it down.

Don't let it escape.

The word *optimism* comes from the Latin *optimum*, meaning "best." What then is an optimist? It's an individual who embraces the following practices:

See the Best

In other words, we look for the good in every person we meet and every situation we face. We are surrounded by beauty and goodness. Distracting as life's negatives can be, we dismiss them as quickly as possible and don't even notice many. Yes, there are certainly plenty of bad and hurtful things in this fallen world of ours, but there are also wonders, miracles, and great beauty. How sad if we allow ourselves to become so overwhelmed by the bad things that we're blinded to the good!

Believe the Best

If we anticipate the best, there's a chance it will happen. This is the core of faith. As Pamela Reeve writes, "Faith is…reliance on the certainty that God has a pattern for my life when everything seems meaningless." Faith believes that God is in control and that His ways are good. Helmet Thielicke was a faithful pastor who was persecuted in Nazi Germany for refusing to renounce his faith. He wrote, "Nothing will be allowed to touch me which has not passed his scrutiny so that it will serve my best interests." Believing the best allows us to see the best.

Choose the Best

Optimism is ultimately a choice. We can choose to reject or embrace it. Our contentment is not determined by our circumstances; it is decided by our choices. A lot of men make poor choices—to be angry, bitter, retaliatory, unhappy, or negative. The reality is that if you don't intentionally choose the best, you will be left with the worst. So as for me, I choose to be positive and optimistic. I choose laughter and fun. I choose joy and hope. I choose life, and I choose to live it to the fullest.

Live the Best

This means walking in faith and trusting God. As David sang, "My soul finds rest in God alone" (Psalm 62:1, NIV). Living close to God is life at its very best. He promises us joy, peace, strength, hope, and comfort. What could be better? God will make your life shine. As Mary Gardiner Brainard insisted, "I would rather walk with God in the dark than go alone in the light."

Optimism can be learned and developed, pursued and embraced. And in so doing we will find the truth and reality of David's prayer: "You have made known to me the path of life; you will fill me with joy in your presence, with eternal pleasures at your right hand" (Psalm 16:11, NIV).

THANK GOD FOR GROWTH

Rejoicing in all that is good. That's a thankful heart, and it can't help but smile. Mother Teresa, in the midst of all the pain and suffering in the poorest back alleys of India, said, "The best way to show my gratitude to God is to accept everything, even my problems, with joy."

Gratitude lifts us above the negativity and mediocrity of life. It energizes us and excites us and infuses us with joy. If we were to review each day everything we have to be thankful for, the practice would soon change our attitude. Thankfulness flows from a daily awareness of God's hand on our shoulder. The suffering may be hard, but His tender mercies are real. With this awareness, we can join the apostle Paul "and always be thankful" (Colossians 3:15).

Robert Jonas could have been angry, bitter, negative. His daughter, Rebecca, was born prematurely and was too fragile even to open her little eyes. He wept and begged God to save this beautiful infant. Rebecca lived for three hours and forty-four minutes. Then she died silently in her father's arms. Robert grieved, but he refused to stay there. Instead of regretting the brevity of Rebecca's life, he chose to thank God for the time she had, as short as it was. He decided to celebrate her life and let his grief lead him to gratitude.

It's easy to thank God for the good times, but it's much more important to thank Him for the difficult times. It is through our wounds that we grow. Thanking God for them moves us forward and brightens our perspective. An optimist has learned the joy of thankfulness. He doesn't ignore the difficulties; he just looks beyond them to see the mighty hand of God. Once we achieve gratitude, we know we have overcome the darkness of our wounds. Truly grateful people can't be stopped.

A NEW SONG

Prison is rarely a positive place to be. Yet Alexander Solzhenitsyn wrote, "It was only when I lay there on a rotting prison floor that I sensed within myself the first stirrings of good...so, bless you, prison, for having been in my life." Alexander refused to let prison crush him.

Nicolaie Moldova, a poet and composer, also experienced the brutality of the Russian prison system.

"Lie on your belly!" a guard yelled to Nicolaie.

The prisoner dropped to the icy cold floor, knowing that the torture would be excruciating. Yet Nicolaie had a plan. The guards then marched on his back, legs, and feet with their heavy boots for the next hour.

They left Nicolaie badly bruised and bleeding. His fellow prisoners rushed to his side, deeply concerned about his condition. Nicolaie raised his head. "I have written a new hymn while I was being walked upon." Then he began to sing, "May I not only speak about future heavens, but let me have heaven and a holy feast here."

After Nicolaie was released from prison, the communist police went through his home and confiscated manuscripts that he had been working on for several years. Much of his lifework was gone, but Nicolaie would not let this loss stop him. He sat down and composed another hymn: "I worship you with gratitude for all you ever gave me, but also for everything beloved you took from me. You do all things well, and I will trust you."

Nicolaie Moldova could have been a victim, but he learned the same lesson as Ron Heagy: Life is an attitude. He had a battle plan. He chose to look up, instead of being pulled down. He decided to cry out to God. Now his songs are sung throughout Russia.

God gave Nicolaie a new song. Some three thousand years earlier, He did the same thing for King David. "I waited patiently for the LORD to help me, and he turned to me and heard my cry. He lifted me out of the pit of despair, out of the mud and the mire. He set my feet on solid ground and steadied me as I walked along. He has given me a new song to sing" (Psalm 40:1–3).

God wants to give us a new song, too. All we have to do is be willing to sing it. That's what winning the battle is all about. That's overcoming. That's optimism.

That's trusting that God knows what He's doing.

CHAPTER 8

LANDMINES

GEORGE HATED HIS LIFE!

All the other guys played sports and enjoyed popularity. George was clumsy and overweight. The kids at school made fun of him. The alienation caused him to eat more, and his weight gain made him feel even more inadequate. His parents forbade sweets; he snuck them. His doctor put him on a diet; he cheated. He felt like a hopeless failure. Nothing worked, and the ridicule and rejection grew even worse.

Angry and depressed, George told his family how miserable he was. Life was cruel, and at various times he blamed his parents, his doctors, his friends. Even God.

During his high school years his weight dropped and schoolmates reached out to him. But his attitude had grown bitter and negative. Everything in his life had to be perfect; he had to be in complete control. He didn't trust anybody. George pushed everyone away and then complained how judgmental and self-absorbed people were for not being his friends.

"If God hadn't given me a weight problem, I wouldn't be so miserable," he said.

"George, you have done a great job of dealing with your weight," I told him. "That's not what is making you miserable. Not now. It's your attitude."

Wounds create pain and darkness, but the pain can be eased and the darkness can be chased away by the light. Yet each wound plants five potential landmines in our life. These bombs can do great damage to our hearts. They can explode in our faces, destroy our positive attitudes, and rip our lives apart. They can cripple us without warning, leaving us more wounded than when we began. We must search our emotional and intellectual world to remove these hazards.

George's wounds made his life difficult, but what hurt him most were the landmines he stepped on. We can avoid these bombs. Or if they've already been planted, we can defuse them. Or if they've exploded, we can reverse their damage. But we have to be willing.

As I spoke to George, it was clear that he had survived his original wounds, but the mental landmines were killing him. Let's look at five attitudes that can sabotage the progress we've made, and keep our wounds fresh and raw.

LANDMINE #1: COMPARISON

We can always find someone who has it easier, looks better, is more athletic, or was blessed in some way that we weren't.

Somebody always owns a better, newer, or more attractive toy. When we are wounded, *everybody* seems happier and stronger. The more we compare, the less satisfied we feel.

Comparisons only make us feel more inadequate. They steal our energy, undermine our morale, and place one more weight on shoulders already bent and burdened. Our wounds do not make us inferior, but often they cause us to *feel* inferior.

The truth is, we are all unique; each of us has both amazing strengths and frustrating weaknesses. Comparison raises three problems. First, we usually compare our weakness with another's strength, leading us to a skewed apples-and-oranges conclusion. Second, what we believe we see in someone else might not be reality! We tend to exaggerate and overestimate the strengths of others. Finally—and please hear this—*our weaknesses and shortcomings, though painful, carry secret treasures and strengths which could be gained no other way.*

Comparisons accomplish nothing positive.

In the church at Corinth, the apostle Paul found himself dealing with a whole clique of comparison junkies. In his letter to that church, Paul asserted, "When they measure themselves by themselves and compare themselves with themselves, they are not wise" (2 Corinthians 10:12, NIV).

God made us who we are, and He remains intimately aware of our circumstances, down to the tiniest detail. No matter what our difficulty, He will guide and walk with us on life's pathway. David wrote, "Every day of my life was recorded in your book. Every moment was laid out" (Psalm 139:16). To compare is to say, "God, I think you messed up here." We are each valued in His eyes, and our wounds *increase* our value. As Billy Graham once said, "Comfort and prosperity have never enriched the world as much as adversity has."

So here are eight things that aren't worth comparing:

- Accomplishments: what others have done
- Success: how well others do
- Intelligence: how smart others are
- Stuff: what others own
- Appearance: how good others look
- Respect: how highly others are thought of
- Circumstances: what blessings others have
- Talents: what abilities or strengths others have

Even if we don't compare, we are frequently surrounded by those who do. We may fear that people are constantly putting us in the balance. Some of our fears are invalid, based on insecurity and paranoia. Yet there are times we are really being compared. People like to practice pigeonholing, matching up one individual against another. It's neither right nor fair nor healthy, but that doesn't stop them. When we are already wounded, we usually assume we're on the negative end of these comparisons.

But the pigeonholers don't know the whole story, do they? In fact, most of the time they don't know very much at all. They don't have all the facts, and they haven't walked in our shoes. God, however, does have all the facts. And in a sense, Jesus walked in our shoes when He became a man and hiked the dusty back roads of planet earth. God doesn't compare. He is a wiser Father than that. He accepts and loves us for who we are—wounds, weakness, and all.

LANDMINE #2: COMPLAINING

Life rarely unfolds the way we wish. Reality has a way of deflating our highly inflated dreams. And what happens when things go wrong (as they inevitably will)?

Sometimes we complain.

We often feel cheated, ripped-off, or taken advantage of. We men find this unacceptable. We will not allow this to continue, so we proclaim the injustice to the world. We just can't take it anymore. We expected things to go differently. We expected life to be smoother or fairer or just a whole lot kinder. In times like these, it's hard to keep our mouths shut.

When we've been wounded, it's easy to feel we're entitled to some special treatment. Special handling. Like the world owes us something. Since we have suffered, we may believe that we deserve something good to compensate for all the bad. People should treat us with more respect and consideration.

They should give us a break. They shouldn't expect as much out of us.

If we don't get what we think we're entitled to, we complain.

What a snare this attitude can become! The plain unvarnished truth is that, wounded or not, *we're not entitled to anything*. That statement may fly in the face of political correctness, but it is absolutely true. Life is a gift, and all that is good is a gift. Entitlement is a false and selfish reality—a narrow pathway that plunges steeply into bitterness.

Besides that, complaining is simply rude and unnecessary.

In fact, it's downright ugly.

It promotes negativity, self-pity, unhappiness, and discord. Complaints cloud the mind and raise the blood pressure. Problems don't have to lead to complaining, but complaining frequently leads to problems. Rather than feeling better about venting, the complainer feels worse, and life's difficulties begin to look more overwhelming than they really are.

Let's face it, we can always find something to complain about. But maturity knows how to stay silent when life doesn't go well. It knows that life is full of hurts and frustrations. It also knows that complaints keep us focused on the problems, rather than the solutions. Anthony J. D'Angelo wrote, "If you have time to whine and complain about something, then you have the time to do something about it."

Complaining keeps us from moving forward and reclaiming our emotional and spiritual health. It ignores what we have and reminds us of what we lack. It keeps us wounded and traps us in self-pity. In order to grow, we must follow the apostle Paul's direction: "Do everything without complaining" (Philippians 2:14, NIV).

LANDMINE #3: CRITICISM

Criticism is the ugly step-sister of complaining. If complaining makes us unhappy and negative, then criticism makes us miserable and bitter. Criticism tears down. It looks for what's wrong and gets so focused on the wrong that anything right or good or positive is minimized. The critic exaggerates a small shadow until it looms so large that he can no longer see the sun. A critical spirit hardens our heart, deepens our wound, and pushes people away. An old proverb says, "The one who is critical walks alone."

Criticism is yet another boomerang: Whatever we throw out will ultimately return to us. Another way to say it is: "Those who criticize, will be criticized." *Even if the criticism is accurate, it rarely accomplishes anything good.*

We usually criticize for one of the following four reasons:

- *To show disapproval*: We don't like something or something doesn't seem fair, so we want the world to know our opinion.
- *To place blame*: We don't want anybody to be angry with us, lose respect for us, or think less of us, so we blame someone else.

- *To feel better*: We feel inferior or insecure, so we find fault with others in order to look better by contrast.
- *To gain power*: We feel powerless or out of control, so we try to appear as if we know more or are superior.

No matter what our motive for criticizing others, it never gets us what we really want. If we show our disapproval, people see us as petty. If we place blame, people believe we're judgmental. If we use this strategy to feel better, people consider us selfish or shallow. If we seek to gain power, people see us as arrogant.

A critical spirit will stunt and blight the growth of a healthy attitude.

The opposite of criticism is praise, or encouragement. If we have been generous with our criticism and stingy with our praise, then our very happiness and health will require us to turn that situation on its head. Paul writes, "Encourage each other and build each other up" (1 Thessalonians 5:11). In so doing, we become stronger and healthier.

It's hard to describe what an impact this truth can have in our homes. Sharp words can destroy a family. As men, we frequently don't realize the power of our words. Please hear this: *Nothing* tears down a marriage or family like criticism, and *nothing* builds and restores it like words of encouragement and praise.

H. Jackson Brown, Jr., provides wise advice when he says, "Let the refining and improving of your own life keep you so busy that you have little time to criticize others."

LANDMINE #4: CYNICISM

Cynical people paint a tragic self-portrait. So sad and miserable that they rarely smile, these unhappy women and men become blind to joy or beauty or wonder—even when it's right before their eyes.

Cynicism is a form of suicide—a slow, painful, and totally avoidable form of death. A cynic is an individual who holds so tightly to his own wounds that he becomes poisoned. The resulting bitterness, like an aggressive cancer, grows and expands until it takes over every aspect of our being—emotionally, intellectually, socially, spiritually, and even physically.

Cynical people see life as...

depressing.

hopeless.

cruel.

painful.

threatening.

unfair.

disappointing.

frightening.

dangerous.

negative.

Ron was verbally abused by his mother. His college girl-friend was unfaithful. After one year of marriage, he came home to find his wife in bed with one his coworkers. Ron was shattered. Ten years later his wound has turned him bitter. He has a love-hate relationship with a number of women and doesn't trust anyone. He is thirty-two, but looks fifty. He wears a constant scowl, and his words cut like a blade. When I asked what might make things better, he replied, "Women? You can't live with them and you can't live without them. Relationships are a pain and life is a joke. It all starts out bad, and every day it gets worse. Nothing can make things better."

Ron is wrong. Things can get better.

But if men get stuck in the ruts of comparison, complaining, or criticism, sooner or later cynicism will grow like weeds in rainy weather. To the cynic everything is a problem with no achievable solution. Small problems loom as insurmountable obstacles. Everything appears bad. And changes? Why, they'll only make things worse! Everybody is incompetent, dangerous, or a personal threat of some sort.

Cynicism is a poison, and even a little bit of it can make you sick. Paul told us to "get rid of all bitterness" (Ephesians 4:31), because he knew that bitterness is the root of cynicism.

Like a good physician, however, the apostle not only identified the symptoms and the disease—he also prescribed good medicine. In his letter to the Philippians, he wrote, "Fix your thoughts on what is true and honorable and right.

Think about things that are pure and lovely and admirable. Think about things that are excellent and worthy of praise" (4:8).

Remember, with God there is *always* hope.

LANDMINE #5: COMPULSIVITY

Many wounded warriors cover their wounds with perfectionism. "When I feel overwhelmed, I've got to make sure everything is in its proper order," said Stu. "It helps me feel in control if everything is scheduled and happens as it should. If anything goes wrong, I can feel myself starting to freak out."

If we can make everything appear perfect, it distracts us from our inner pain. We compulsively work on polishing the surface of life, so the broken and imperfect core doesn't show through. In many ways this is the opposite of cynicism, which sees everything as negative and has given up. Compulsivity is driven to make everything, not just positive, but *perfect*. It refuses to give up. In every comparison, it strives to be the best. Its complaining or criticism is not aimed toward others; it's aimed toward oneself. Nothing one does is good enough unless it's perfect.

The goals of compulsive behavior are simple. Simple and impossible.

Perfect grades.

Perfect composure.

Perfect job.

Perfect attitude.

Perfect performance.

Perfect wife.

Perfect family.

Perfect house.

The compulsive person believes he has failed if everything is not "just right." He is easily disappointed, because things rarely turn out as well as he would like. Much of this compulsivity and perfectionism is based upon fear.

- Fear of rejection
- Fear of failure
- Fear of being found out
- Fear of disappointing others

These fears keep us driven toward the unattainable and set us up for failure. Here are a few ways to avoid this landmine.

Admit that perfectionism is impossible.

No one is perfect and nothing we do will be perfect. Perfect Tens don't exist anywhere outside of Hollywood fantasy. We are damaged, and that's reality. The more we try to cover up a wound, the more frustrated, exhausted, and defeated we will feel. Besides, perfectionists make most of us nervous. They don't seem real; we can't relate to them. And who can relax and kick back in a house where the couch cushions have no wrinkles, everything is flawlessly in place, and not even a speck of dust rests on a single surface?

Give ourselves permission to make mistakes.

We must all accept that mistakes and stumbles are a part of life. Making a mistake does not mean we are failures. Expectations of a mistake-free life are unrealistic, absurd. We all make mistakes every day. Rather than flailing ourselves, we can all challenge ourselves to do a little better tomorrow than we did yesterday.

Accept our strengths and weaknesses.

We all have areas that we excel in and areas in which we inevitably fall flat on our face. We don't need to pretend we have it all together, because we don't and we never will. *But that's okay.* We can celebrate our strengths and lean on others to help us cope with those irritating and sometimes embarrassing weaknesses.

Recognize that our wounds create limitations.

Wounds leave scars. Wounds create limps. Certain things would be easier if our hurts had never happened. To act as if our wounds are irrelevant is foolish. Yet to give up as a result of them is equally foolish. In most situations there are specific things we can do to minimize the limitations our wounds cause. But the healthy choice is to swallow our pride and seek help from friends, pastors, counselors, organizations, books—or from whatever source our compassionate Lord provides.

Do our realistic best.

Doing things well is important. But there is nothing more discouraging than attempting to do what can't be done. While a perfect job is impossible, most of us can do a *good* job if we put in the time and effort. As a counselor, I encourage people to do the best they can without putting themselves down for falling short of perfection.

DEFUSING THE LANDMINES

Don't minimize the danger of these five lethal landmines! Triggering them can unleash deadly negative force, blasting and shattering hopes of healing and happiness, imprisoning people behind iron bars of bitterness.

Ironically, it's rarely our wounds that cripple or destroy us. It's the aftermath—*how we handle the lingering landmines*—that can have deadly potential. If we are intentional, we can step around them. If we are careful, we can defuse them.

The presence of landmines does not mean there must be an explosion. Yet it does mean that we must keep our eyes wide open. We must guard our hearts. Solomon issued this warning: "Above all else, guard your heart, for it affects everything you do" (Proverbs 4:23).

Amy Carmichael was born in Northern Ireland in 1867. At an early age she felt called to help the poor, and in spite of struggles with her health, this feeling grew more compelling with age. When she was twenty-eight, she packed up and moved to Dohnavur in southern India. There she saved over a thousand children from horrific lives as temple prostitutes.

One day as Amy was praying, she felt that God was preparing her for some sort of expanded impact. So she prayed, "God use me in a greater way so Thy will may come to pass." The next day she fell, breaking her leg and injuring her spine. For the rest of her life, Amy was confined to her bed. Yet instead of comparing or complaining or becoming cynical, Amy saw this as a new opportunity.

During the next twenty years, Amy Carmichael enjoyed the gift of time to write. That's when she penned some of her most powerful and influential books. These works spread her impact beyond India and beyond her lifetime. In the midst of this painful confinement she wrote, "Let us not be surprised when we have to face difficulties. When the wind blows hard on a tree, the roots stretch and grow stronger. Let it be so with me."

We cannot control most of the wounds that mark our lives, but we can defuse the landmines that accompany them. A healthy person can have no part of comparisons, complaining, criticism, cynicism, or compulsion. These only exaggerate our wounds and increase our limitations. So push away the dark clouds and defuse the landmines. In so doing we learn the truth in the words of John Wooden: "Things turn out best for the people who make the best of the way things turn out."

CHAPTER 9
FELLOW SOLDIERS

I NEVER REALLY KNEW PAUL.

He owned a little deli next door to my office and served the best hot pastrami sandwich I'd ever had in my life. I'd go in and we'd chat about our kids. We were friendly, but we never talked deep. I'd see him on the soccer field with his son and at dance recitals with his daughter. He would smile; we would make small talk and say we ought to get together sometime and get to know each other better.

The last time I saw Paul, he told me life was tough. His deli was losing money and things weren't going well at home. He said, "Dr. Steve, I ought to make an appointment and talk to you about some things that are really bothering me." I told him that he could call me anytime.

Paul never called. Two days later I dropped into his deli, but Paul wasn't there. The deli was unusually quiet and the help looked downcast. "Where's Paul?" I asked cheerfully.

"Oh, you haven't heard?" said the young lady behind the counter. "Paul shot himself last night. He died instantly."

I couldn't believe it. Why would he kill himself? Why didn't he talk to someone? Why hadn't I asked more questions when he mentioned his hardships?

Paul needed to talk. He needed friends. He needed help. Yet Paul was like most of us guys: We smile, work hard, and pretend everything is okay, even if everything is falling apart on the inside. Paul tried to reach out to me the last time I saw him, but I didn't recognize his real need. Now it's too late and I'm left wishing I'd gotten to know Paul better.

As guys, we are not good at reaching out, or noticing when someone else is reaching out. We tend to keep to ourselves. We retreat, we stay late at work, we sit hypnotized by television, we become obsessed with sports, we go to the garage, we take a drive, we dive into projects. These are all subconscious ways of isolating from others. As one man once told me, "Isolation is totally comfortable to me."

We need people the most when we're wounded. But that's when we tend to become most detached.

Here are ten reasons that men isolate themselves:

1. We are angry or disappointed because people don't meet our expectations.
2. We don't know how to reach out and we would feel foolish asking for help.
3. We feel inadequate because we don't believe it's acceptable for men to be wounded.

4. We are in crisis, and we believe we must deal with it ourselves.

5. We have seen that people can be dangerous and feel we must protect ourselves.

6. We have experienced a failure of trust and we're suspicious.

7. We must cover up sin or failure because we're embarrassed.

8. We don't know what to do, but we don't want to bother others with our problems.

9. We are stressed, overwhelmed, or confused, but we think if we just give it enough time we can figure it out or it will just go away.

10. We feel we can't risk exposure because we fear rejection or loss of respect.

We all need fellow soldiers. It's no fun to fight and march and work alone. Sure we can manage by ourselves. We are men; we can do anything. Yet we need friends—people who really care, people we can count on.

Too many men report that they have no close friends whom they can truly trust. They may have acquaintances, neighbors, or colleagues, but no fellow soldiers, no other guy who will stand by them no matter what. No one who might even take a bullet for them if need be. So they go into battle with no one to watch their back.

Life is tough, but life without friends is merciless. Today's warriors are lonely and alone. Too often they fight their foes with no wingman. Too often they fall to the ground with no one to pick them up and carry them back to safety. Wise, experienced soldiers stand back to back or side by side. Unless there is absolutely no other option. Only then, out of desperation, are they forced to stand alone. This is their last resort after every other alternative has failed.

When we are wounded, we feel disconnected from people. Sometimes we want to run away and hide. Though we secretly yearn for people, we don't feel safe with them. We're afraid they will hurt us more. We feel vulnerable, broken, inferior, hypervigilant, insecure.

But mostly, we're just scared.

Though people have hurt us in the past and will probably hurt us again, we still need them. People contact is crucial to our healing and health. To grow we need to learn to trust again by reaching out to others. And allowing them to reach out to us.

Still unconvinced? Here are some reasons we all need people.

KEEPING US COMPANY

"Loneliness," wrote Norman Vincent Peale, "lurks in the shadows of adversity." When we are lonely we feel deserted, abandoned, and secluded. We feel isolated and wonder if anyone "out there" wants to spend time with us. Ironically, when we are wounded we may build walls, keeping others at a distance—even while we yearn with all our hearts for company.

We need people to help us grow and stretch beyond ourselves.

We need people who will share our hopes, fears, and tears.

We need people to laugh with, when life gets too serious and grim.

We need people to love and accept us, so that we might learn to love and accept ourselves.

We need people to pull us out of hiding, that we might stand in the sunshine.

We need company when we've been wounded, but it needs to be *healthy* company. Deep inside we know there's a difference. Seeking help from people opens us up to the possibility of further wounding. If we're more aware of the risk of harm than we are of our need for help, we try to push everyone away, thinking it makes us safer. But we're actually placing ourselves in greater danger.

As wounded warriors, we may become overprotective of our feelings. Since the thought of being hurt again can be almost too much to bear, we become mistrustful—even fearful—of people who try to edge into our world. We build our walls high, seeking maximum shielding from potential pain.

The sad truth is that we *can't* trust everyone we meet. We must be *wise*, reaching out to positive people and building positive relationships, while maintaining healthy boundaries with those who may be dangerous. When we've been wounded, we must find safe friends who...

- Don't shock easily.
- Don't give unwanted advice.
- Remind us of our strengths.
- Believe we can make it through difficult times.
- Accept our weaknesses.
- Respect our courage and sense of determination.
- Try to understand our feelings.
- Pray with us and for us.

Of course, while all of this counsel may *sound* logical, implementing it may prove very, very difficult for people in pain. At certain times in our lives, just contemplating the possibility of opening the blast doors may seem unthinkable. The chore of sifting safe friends from unsafe may feel overwhelming.

In such seasons, God wants us simply to ask Him for the necessary wisdom and let Him guide us. David knew this: "For I am overwhelmed and desperate, and you alone know which way I ought to turn" (Psalm 142:3, TLB).

CARING FOR US

We all have times when we crave encouragement from someone who cares. These are times when life feels at its lowest ebb. Our pain may be so great that we want to give up. The world may seem so dark and empty and cruel that we wonder why we should continue trying. We may want to yell or cry or simply pack up our bags and disappear. How we long for someone to care in that moment…some strong and gentle someone who will lift us out of our fear, depression, anger, guilt, and shame.

Just today I spoke with a man who recently weathered a deep personal crisis. "I was so lonely," he recalled. "Everybody I called wasn't there. All I wanted was someone—anyone—to tell me I'd make it and things would be okay."

That's the way it is when you're in deep emotional pain. You reach out because you feel as though you'll die if you don't. Sometimes someone reaches back, and we are comforted by that contact, even if only for a moment. Other times, the only One who responds is God, drawing us deeper into His embrace than we've ever been before.

Most of the time, however, it pleases the Father to dispense His hope and help through the hearts, hands, and voices of His other sons and daughters. We are to "comfort and encourage each other" (1 Thessalonians 4:18), for these are two of the greatest needs of anyone who is wounded. As people apply these two ointments of grace, our heart softens and our body relaxes. Suddenly we can see beyond our wounds and hear the powerful melodies of a brighter tomorrow.

Comfort and encouragement come in at least three equally powerful packages. Someone's *words* can speak into our life, lifting us out of despair. Saying things like: "You are appreciated!" or "You can do it." or "God is going to use you in great ways."

Words change lives. As Solomon wrote some three thousand years ago, "An encouraging word cheers a person up" (Proverbs 12:25). And again, "Pleasant words are a honeycomb, sweet to the soul and healing to the bones" (Proverbs 16:24, NASB).

Also, a caring *touch* can calm a troubled heart and chase away the cold chill of loneliness. There are times we all need the compassion of human touch—a firm embrace, a solid grip, an arm around our shoulders, a pat on the back. In fact, without these some of us will shrivel and die.

A friend of mine who had lost his middle-aged wife to cancer after twenty-five years of marriage told me that for several months, a few women in the church simply served as huggers in his life. Without embarrassment, without hesitation, without words, without worrying about appearances, these two or three women would simply embrace him for thirty seconds or so. Out of all the kind and generous things that good church did for him through those terrible months of grieving, that physical contact meant more to him than anything else.

Henri Nouwen writes, "When we honestly ask ourselves which person in our lives means the most to us, we often find that it is those who, instead of giving advice, solutions, or cures, have chosen rather to share our pain and touch our wounds with a warm and tender hand."

And then sometimes all we need, or can even accept, is someone's *presence*. Words can be wonderful, but they can also get in the way. Touch can be affirming, but it can also be uncomfortable. Sometimes comfort and encouragement come through most effectively when someone simply stands beside us. A silent, reassuring presence can be among the best gifts we ever give someone. So why is it so hard to give? David Augsburger writes, "It is so much easier to tell a person what to do with his problem than to stand with him in his pain."

When we are crushed or burned out, we might know to connect with others, but we don't know how. Here are a few suggestions for starting out:

1. **Recognize your need.** When life is most difficult, you need people the most. They provide much-needed comfort, encouragement, and perspective.

2. **Take a risk.** It may feel awkward and challenging to connect with others. You may find a hundred reasons to hide inside yourself, but you need to reach out.

3. **Call on an old friend.** You have long-time friends or relatives that you trust. Call one of them, even if you haven't spoken for a while.

4. **Get involved.** Find a cause, a church, a class, a club, or a committee where you'll be in regular contact with others. Then jump in, whether you feel like it or not. Remember, feelings follow actions.

5. **Volunteer.** Get out and help others. Be active. Be social. As you surround yourself with others, you will feel better.

6. **Reduce isolating activities.** Stop spending so much time on solitary activities, such as TV, computers, and video games. Force yourself out of the house.

7. **Don't let yourself fall into self-pity.** It's easy to feel sorry for yourself when you're hurting, but this only makes things worse. When you focus on the pain too much, it pushes others away.

8. **Ask God for direction.** Pray that God will provide a name, an idea, or an opportunity to make a positive personal connection.

HELPING US GROW

We are most open to growth after we have hit bottom in our lives. In those moments we realize that Band-Aid approaches and watered-down remedies simply won't cut it. Truly desperate, we realize that we cannot emerge from our painful despair on our own.

When we are too close to our pain and problems, we frequently can't find a way out—even if it's right in front of us. This doesn't mean we're stupid or incompetent. All it means is that we are blinded by our wounds and our pain. We need someone with a more objective perspective or greater life experience to come alongside us and lead us to a better place.

In a perfect world these people come to us.

In a perfect world, caring people would see us in desperate need and rush to our aid.

But as we all know, our world is far from perfect. Besides, we men are great at hiding our wounds. Therefore, instead of expecting people to be drawn to us in our difficulty and sorrow, we must go to them. We must seek wise, grace-filled, positive people to guide, direct, counsel, coach, teach, advise, or mentor us. This helps us move toward healing and protects us from inadvertently suffering further wounds. As Solomon wrote, "Plans fail for lack of counsel, but with many advisers they succeed" (Proverbs 15:22, NIV).

You want to grow and be all God knows you can be. Don't let pride or embarrassment keep you from getting the help you need. We can always use help, and we always need to grow. But when we are wounded, such help is nothing short of crucial. Even though it may seem elusive, even though we may not find it as readily as we hope, help is worth seeking.

And keep in mind: Right now you may be the one needing encouragement, but tomorrow you may be the one offering a helping hand. If you won't let anyone pull you up, how will you have the emotional footing to help the next man?

We guys frequently need coaching. We can find ourselves in over our head; we might need a different perspective.

Yet we often resist assistance, advice, or counseling. We want to do it our way. But coaching multiplies the possibilities.

We've seen it a hundred times: An average team with a great coach can do amazing things. We all can learn more, go further, reach higher, and become more successful when properly coached. Every man needs a life coach. A skilled guide can help you...

- build communication skills.
- solve problems.
- improve relationships.
- set goals.
- challenge negative thinking.
- identify self-destructive patterns.
- nurture spiritual growth.
- promote maturity.
- celebrate personal strengths and potential.
- strengthen character.

PRAYING FOR US

When we know people are praying for us, whether they are standing right next to us or are halfway around the world, it helps ease our pain. When someone prays for us, they invite God to touch us. Bruce Wilkinson writes, "Prayer is a path to God's blessing." Prayer is the solution to every problem. It recognizes God's hand on our shoulder, and reminds us that He has not forgotten us. I love it when Paul tells his friend Timothy, "Night and day I constantly remember you in my prayers" (2 Timothy 1:3). What a connection! What an encouragement!

Prayer reminds us that this is a supernatural world and that God is close at hand. All we need to do is cry out. Prayer leads to greater results than we can ever imagine. In response to prayer, God provides direction, strength, and ultimately peace. Knowing that people are praying for us gives us encouragement and comfort. When our wounds are deep, it is sometimes hard to pray. Yet knowing that someone is seeking God on our behalf—filling the gap, saying what we can't, asking for God's intervention—keeps our connection with the source of hope and health alive.

When someone prays with us or for us, they invite God into our life. As Oswald Chambers wrote, "God comes where my helplessness begins." We know how desperately we need God's help. Yet when the pain is great, we sometimes feel that He is distant. Our prayers seem to fall short of their goal, and our words feel like wasted breath. In times like these we long for someone to intercede for us and plead our case. We need someone to provide that extra push of prayer to get us started. We want to cry out like David, "Please, God, rescue me! Come quickly, LORD, and help me" (Psalm 70:1). But our prayer efforts end up as meaningless mumbles. However, when someone else cries out on our behalf, we can add our amen, and the fog seems to clear.

Every day someone asks me directly or via phone to pray for them. Some people ask boldly, others with hesitation or fear. No matter how hectic or busy my day might be, I consider it a great privilege to pray with or for someone.

There is no power in the universe greater than the power of God.

There is no love in all of creation greater than the love of God.

And there is no one anywhere who cares more about the most minute details of our lives than God. *He* is the One to whom we bring our wounded friends. And He is the One who will touch us in the deepest places of our pain and bring healing as others pray for us. What a mighty force! It connects us with each other and with the Master of the universe. Without prayer we are disconnected from our hope.

So we all need to ask for prayer and uphold others with a steady, heartfelt habit of prayer. As an old saying so aptly puts it, "Prayer is the key to the morning and the bolt at night."

GIVING BACK TO OTHERS

Tom was on his fourth marriage when I called him and asked if he would be a marriage mentor to a newlywed couple.

He laughed. "Dr. Steve, is this a joke? You know my history. Why in the world are you asking me?"

"I thought you'd be a great mentor," I told him. "You and Sally have been married twelve years, and you know firsthand the pain of failed marriages. So tell me, Tom, what *have* you learned from your divorces?"

Tom hesitated a moment before he spoke. "Well… I've learned that you have to be committed. And not get so upset when things don't go your way. I've learned that if you don't work at it every day, it can fall apart. But if you do work at it, things will get better."

"And that's what I want you to teach this young couple."

Giving back to others gives our wounds meaning. It connects us with others as mentor and coach, rather than leaving us in isolation as a victim. When Henri Nouwen speaks of "the wounded healer," he hits on a powerful paradox that gives us all hope. For it is because of our wounds that we can frequently give the most genuine and life-changing help. So as we reach out, let us stay in contact with others, help our brothers who are in trouble, and be patient with everyone.

I recently heard a story about a man and woman who had both lost their spouses to cancer. As the man described his loneliness and pain, the woman began to weep uncontrollably. Soon he placed his arm around her, and they wept together.

It's easy for our wounds to cause us to withdraw into isolation, self-pity, and protection. Yet this is a terrible waste of our experience. Paul wrote, "When God comforts us, it is so that we, in turn, can be an encouragement to you" (2 Corinthians 1:6).

I think of Lonnie who works with troubled teens, John who volunteers at a homeless shelter, and Craig who leads

For Men Only groups on sexual addictions. Why do these men do what they do? It's because they've been on the other side. But they're not just bringing encouragement and wisdom into the lives of other boys and men; they're reaping some rich benefits of their own. Flora Edwards once said, "In helping others, we shall help ourselves, for whatever good we give out completes the circle and comes back to us."

NEEDING OTHER SOLDIERS

Our wounds force us to face our need for one another. We all need someone to lean on, someone who will stand beside us and try to understand. We need people who will love us, and whom we can love back. A world without friendships is cold and lonely.

Throughout Scripture, our greatest heroes surrounded themselves with others. Moses had Aaron, Joshua had Caleb. David had Jonathan and seventy mighty men. Elijah had Elisha. Jesus had his twelve disciples. Paul had Timothy, Titus, and a company of others. God's Word consistently reminds us that we are better together than we are alone.

The poet Samuel Taylor Coleridge once wrote that "friendship is a sheltering tree." On a hot summer's day it shades us, and on a blustery winter's night it protects us from the storm. We all are strengthened by those who stand around us. Their smiles make us smile and their encouragement keeps us from giving up. My best times are with people because, as

John Eldridge writes in *Waking the Dead*, when we are together "we hear each other's stories. We discover each other's glories. We learn to walk with God together. We pray for each other's healing. We cover each other's back."

If our lives went perfectly, we might become so self-sufficient and independent that we wouldn't need others. Our lives aren't perfect. Neither are we. Chuck Swindoll reminds us that "tucked away in a quiet corner of every life are wounds and scars. If they were not there, we would need no Physician. Nor would we need one another."

So let's not fight it; let's just admit we're all broken. Only then can we truly help each other through the hard times. Only then can we celebrate with each other when all goes well.

FRIENDLY FIRE AND SELF-INFLICTED WOUNDS

CHAPTER 10

SOME MOVIES ARE BRUTAL.

In the 2001 movie *Black Hawk Down*, a U. S. helicopter is shot down in the heart of Somalia's capital city, territory held by a crime lord and his army. American soldiers try to get in to rescue those in the chopper, but the firefight is heavy. The rescue turns into a disaster as guerrilla forces spray the soldiers with machine gun fire from every direction. The battle is bloody. A cargo truck moves in and loads up with wounded American soldiers. The officer in charge commands one of his men to get into the truck and drive it back to the military base.

"I can't," the soldier says. "I'm shot."

The officer looks at the soldier and yells, "We're all shot. Get in and drive!"

We're all wounded and we are all brothers. That's the human condition. But life continues and we have to keep on going anyway. No matter how bloodied and battered, warriors don't give up.

I can handle most wounds, but there are two that cut me to the quick, that strike with greater intensity than most. They are friendly fire and self-inflicted wounds.

FRIENDLY FIRE

Pat Tillman's dreams had come true. He had a $3.6 million contract with the Arizona Cardinals pro football team, for whom he played starting safety. Then came the September 11 World Trade Center attack. At the age of twenty-five, Tillman walked away from his dream to serve his country as a U. S. Army Ranger.

On April 22, 2004, Tillman participated in Operation Mountain Storm in rugged and remote terrain in eastern Afghanistan near the Pakistan border. At about seven-thirty that evening Tillman's platoon was ambushed. For the next twenty minutes an intense and confusing firefight ensued involving mortars, small arms, and a land mine. When the smoke cleared, Pat Tillman's friends discovered that he had been shot and killed. Exactly what happened is hazy, but one thing is definite: Tillman had been shot by his own men. It was a case of friendly fire. It was clearly accidental, but no less deadly.

It often happens in combat, but in day-to-day life it shouldn't be that common. Unfortunately it is. Nothing seems so painful to me as when those I trust or think I should be able to trust stab me in the back. I seldom succumb to depression, but for one exception: friendly fire. Somehow it takes the wind out of my sails and leaves me floundering. Maybe this is because I'm an optimist and yearn to believe the best of people. It seems incomprehensible that friends and relatives—especially true Christians—would want to wound me. Why would they? If I treat people with kindness and fairness, won't they treat me the same way? I still struggle over experiences that answer this question with a resounding "No!"

People can be cold and cruel. My mind fights to deny this, but my experience says it's true. I don't want to admit that Jeremiah was right when he wrote, "The human heart is most deceitful and desperately wicked" (Jeremiah 17:9). How can you keep from growing cynical when you know people who...

- assume the worst about you.
- kick you when you're down.
- won't forgive you.
- refuse to talk to you.
- gossip or slander you.
- indicate you aren't good enough.
- ignore or minimize you.
- cheat, lie, or take advantage of you.
- break your confidence.
- say hurtful things.
- embarrass or humiliate you.
- show no compassion.

Yet I'm glad to point out that for every one person who has done any of the above, I know at least fifty who have not. Most people I know are good, but it takes just one to leave me reeling.

Abraham Lincoln was not a happy man. His mother died when he was nine. He had a difficult relationship with his father. He struggled to find a successful career. At the age of thirty-one, Lincoln considered himself a failure. He fell into a deep depression and wrote, "I am now the most miserable man living." Things only got worse.

Lincoln went on to marry, and his wife nagged, harassed, ridiculed, and embarrassed him for nearly twenty-five years. In 1862, his son died. In 1863, the startling number of Civil War casualties haunted him. That summer he read through the book of Job and identified with its namesake. He wrote, "I can hardly see a ray of hope," and those who knew him described him as a "complete picture of dejection."

All of this was devastating, but what crushed him most was what he called the "treachery of false friends." Throughout Lincoln's presidency, Horace Greeley, editor of the powerful *New York Tribune* and supposed friend, disagreed with many of Lincoln's policies. He wrote brutal, bitter, sarcastic, personal attacks on the president right up to the night of his assassination. The rejection and loneliness was oppressive. As one writer observed, "He could bear defeat inflicted by his enemies with pretty good grace, but it was hard to be wounded in the house of his friends."

Friendly fire can crush you. When people you trust attack, it can be earth-shattering. But we are all capable of mean behavior. We have each had our cruel moments. We are all selfish, and in certain situations we have just as much potential for delivering friendly fire as anyone else. This is particularly true if the situation involves power, money, ego, comfort, reputation, or position. Men have a tendency to protect themselves. If we believe someone is blocking our goal, we push harder. We want to win, even if it means running over a friend.

Jesus presented a different way. But it requires us to swallow our pride and self-interest. We have to treat people the same way we'd like them to treat us. He said, "The greatest among you must be a servant. But those who exalt themselves will be humbled, and those who humble themselves will be exalted" (Matthew 23:11–12). Jesus was saying that in order to win we must let go of power, money, ego, comfort, reputation, and position. Only then can we be servants.

Reaching out to others unselfishly should be easy, but people so often give in to that malicious side. It perplexes me, that tendency to kick someone when they're down.

No one has had a day quite like the one Job had. In a single day his business was destroyed, his assets stolen, his employees massacred, and all his children killed. Shortly after this Job was struck "with a terrible case of boils from head to foot." Job was depressed. His wife's suggestion: "Curse God and die."

Three of his friends came "to comfort and console him." They sat on the ground with him for seven days and seven nights. They didn't say anything, "for they saw that his suffering was too great for words." They started out so well. But then they started sharing their opinions. They began to criticize and argue with Job. Their attempts to help only made things worse. Job even cried out, "What miserable comforters you are!"

These men were insensitive, negative, accusatory, and arrogant. They came with good intentions, but their egos got in the way. They didn't understand Job and were so busy articulating their opinions that they didn't truly listen. Their words and judgments caused Job further injury. Friendly fire. (See the book of Job, especially chapters 1–2 and 16:2.)

When men are freshly wounded, it's important that our "help" doesn't deepen the wound. Here are some words *not* to say:

- "It's not as bad as it looks."
- "I know how you feel."
- "God is building something great in you."
- "Things will be better in a few months."
- "God will work it all out for good."
- "You have to move on."
- "Give it to God and everything will be better."
- "Feeling sorry for yourself doesn't help anything."

All of these words may be true, but when a person's pain is fresh, certain words come across as insensitive and cruel. After all, we don't want to be like Job's friends who ended up shooting their wounded.

There are two sides to every story. At times we may be Job's friends and at other times we are Job. If we are caught in friendly fire, what do we do? Here are a few ideas:

Face your anger, hurt, and disappointment.

Talk to trusted friends and counselors about these feelings.

Avoid isolation, self-pity, bitterness, or revenge; they won't get you anywhere.

Lean on God, knowing that He will never let you down.

Evaluate how you might have prevented or avoided this situation.

Set up boundaries with dangerous people so this doesn't happen again.

Refrain from overgeneralization that sees everybody as potentially dangerous.

Risk giving trust and love again; don't be afraid to build healthy relationships.

Move on with your life so that past hurts become the foundation for future successes.

Make sure you don't become the source of friendly fire in someone else's life.

Implementing these measures will not take away the sting of friendly fire. I'm not sure anything will. But it will help you gain perspective. Friendly fire is nothing new; it has been around since Cain and Abel. Friendly fire is also nothing personal; it tells much more about the one attacking than the one attacked. Friendly fire is one of the most painful wounds that any guy can receive. Yet it can teach powerful lessons. It drove Lincoln to greatness and Job to God. As with anything in this world, God can use friendly fire to strengthen and enrich us.

FORGIVEN TO FORGIVE

"Et tu, Brute?"

These are three of the most famous words uttered in literature.

Marcus Brutus was a distant cousin and good friend to Julius Caesar. In the previous four years Caesar had given Brutus more honor and respect than any other senator. But Brutus grew disenchanted with Caesar's political agenda. Instead of going to his friend and discussing his frustrations, he went behind Caesar's back and complained to the other senators. As he stirred them up, a plot was hatched.

On March 15, 44 BC, Caesar was stabbed twenty-three times in the Roman Senate house. He had dismissed his bodyguards, for he trusted his political colleagues. As he sank to the ground, he saw Brutus, dagger in hand, among his murderers. In agony and disbelief, he spoke his final accusing words: "You too, Brutus?"

This phrase has gone down in history as symbolic of ultimate betrayal by one's closest friend. Seventy-five years after these events, Jesus experienced a similar betrayal as He was praying late one night in an olive grove just south of Jerusalem. Judas led a mob, armed with swords and clubs, to Jesus' haven. Jesus had to be feeling deep pain and disappointment when He said, "Judas, how can you betray me...with a kiss?" (Luke 22:48).

Jesus understands friendly fire. Not only was He betrayed by Judas, but by all humanity. Yet as He dangled in excruciating pain on the rough-hewn timbers of a cross, He pleaded, "Father, forgive these people, because they don't know what they are doing" (Luke 23:34). In the end there is no good excuse for friendly fire, but there is forgiveness. His sacrifice brought us forgiveness; our willingness to forgive can set free those who have attacked us.

SELF-INFLICTED WOUNDS

I don't know how he did it.

Trevor had taken gun safety classes and had always shown guns plenty of respect. Yet somehow his revolver went off as he was holding it at his side. A bullet went through his calf. It was a clean wound, but it hurt like crazy.

Trevor limped for the next six months and had to use a cane. He was young and his wound eventually healed completely. But he has two round scars—an entrance and an exit—to remind him of his self-inflicted wound. Trevor was lucky. Most men with this sort of wound don't get off so easy.

Self-wounds can go deeper than we ever thought possible. Jerry's one-night stand gave him genital herpes. Chuck's gambling took him to bankruptcy. Lonnie's reckless driving killed his best friend in the passenger seat. Ryan's weed habit kept him from graduating from high school. Russell's procrastination cost him his job.

Self-inflicted wounds come in a thousand different shapes—mistakes, miscalculations, unmanaged anger, immaturity, over-confidence, over-reactions, oversights, stupidity, sin, confusion, inconsideration, and fears, to mention just a few. But I've discovered eight most common ways that we set ourselves up for auto-injury.

By isolating ourselves.

When we retreat from people for whatever reason (shame, guilt, anger, mistrust), we block ourselves from sources of perspective and encouragement. As our isolation grows, so does our loneliness and pain.

By not asking for help.

There are times we all need help. Failing to seek help keeps us trapped in a rut, and we repeat our mistakes. As we receive advice or coaching, we become equipped to pull out of negative patterns.

By pretending everything is okay.

We all could improve in some area of our life. To cling to an I've-got-it-all-together attitude is to hide behind either arrogance or denial. When we refuse to acknowledge our weaknesses and needs, we set ourselves up for a fall.

By feeding our addictions.

To escape reality through addictive patterns—such as alcohol, drugs, sex, food, or gambling—only creates new struggles and difficulties, which are frequently worse than the pain we were initially trying to avoid.

By making poor choices.

We have all done or said things about which, in hindsight, we wonder, *What was I thinking?* We are all guilty of naïve, immature, hurtful, foolish, and outright wrong choices. No excuses. But hopefully experience will teach us how to fall into these traps less often.

By not taking responsibility.

When we insist upon blaming others and refuse to recognize our liability for a wound, we blind ourselves to lessons we might learn to avoid re-creating the situation in the future. Unless we accept our mistakes, we cannot learn from them.

By being passive.

Doing nothing makes us victims. Feeling sorry for ourselves makes us tragic victims. When we fall or fail, we must stand up and evaluate what just happened. This way we can develop an active, intentional plan to keep it from happening again.

By not going to God.

To think that we can stay healthy and do the right thing apart from God is naïve. We are far too selfish. Only God can provide protection from avoidable self-wounds. Only God gives direction toward healing when we've just suffered a self-inflicted wound. Only God enables continued healing when we're recovering from self-wounds.

Our thirty-seventh president, Richard M. Nixon, failed in at least six of these areas. His self-inflicted wounds can be summed up in one word: Watergate.

This word brings instantly to mind what might be the top presidential scandal in American history. On June 17, 1972, five burglars were arrested while breaking into the Democratic National Committee's Headquarter at the Watergate office complex in Washington, D.C. During the next two years the FBI discovered that this break-in was funded by the Committee to Reelect the President. White House tapes also revealed that Richard Nixon had ordered a secret cover-up of the break-in as early as six days after the event.

As the facts unfolded, layers of lies, manipulations, bribes, threats, and stalls came to light. Richard Nixon insisted that he was in no way involved, even though the tapes demonstrated just the opposite. By mid-1974, the House of Representatives prepared articles of impeachment involving three particular charges: obstruction of justice, abuse of power, and contempt of Congress.

On August 8, 1974, Richard Nixon became the first and only U.S. president to resign from office. This scandal need not have happened. If only Nixon had considered the consequences.

Life is full of consequences. Every action—big or small, purposeful or accidental—has it consequences. You jump from a building, you fall. You overeat, you gain weight. You don't go to work, you lose your job. Every action has its effect. You may be able to escape consequences for a while, but they will catch up with you. At first certain people may appear to have gotten away with murder, but just wait.

The Bible is full of examples of self-wounds—situations in which people's actions led to severe consequences in their own lives. Here are a few examples:

- Adam broke the rules; he lost his innocence.
- Lot's wife looked back; she lost her life.
- Abraham lied; he almost lost his wife.
- Moses murdered; he lost his home.
- Sampson broke his vow; he lost his strength.
- King Saul got impatient; he lost his throne.
- King David slept with his neighbor; he lost his integrity and his son.
- Peter took his eyes off Jesus; he lost his footing.

No one is immune to self-wounds. As long as we allow ourselves to be tempted by power, ego, money, comfort, reputation, or position, we run the risk of auto-injury. Each of these temptations can consume us and cloud our thinking. Normally rational men then find themselves committing atrocities that, in their clear-minded state, they would think impossible of themselves.

DIVINE HEALING FOR HUMAN FLAWS

They were two of the most brilliant men of their time. They were both aides to George Washington during the Revolutionary War. They were both successful New York City lawyers.

They were avid political enemies.

Aaron Burr was the son of the president of Princeton and grandson of Jonathan Edwards—one of the most famous theologians in America. He became a U.S. Senator and Vice President under Thomas Jefferson. He would probably have become president if Alexander Hamilton hadn't so actively opposed him. Hamilton was an Army general and is considered one of the United States' Founding Fathers. He was the chief author of the Federalist Papers and the first Secretary of the Treasury.

For years the two men had attacked and undermined each other, but in 1804, Hamilton hurt Burr's feelings. Burr was so offended that he challenged Hamilton to an illegal duel. On the morning of July 11, near the shore of the Hudson River at Weehauken, New Jersey, the two men stood ten paces from each other. When the signal was given, each man fired a shot from a .56-caliber dueling pistol at the other.

This became the most famous duel in history. An illegal and arrogant act over a minor slight destroyed both men. Hamilton was hit. He died the next day at the age of forty-nine. Burr was charged with murder and fled for his life. He drifted through the Western Territories of the U.S. and then escaped to Europe. Much of the time he lived on the verge of poverty.

Many years later he returned to New York City, but he could never shake his reputation as the man who shot Alexander Hamilton. He died a rejected and lonely man.

The best way to avoid self-wounds is to think before you act. Talk things through with trusted friends and ask yourself a few questions, such as:

- Is this wise?
- Is this legal?
- Is this right?
- Why am I doing this?
- What are the potential negative consequences?
- Would this please God?

By slowing down and contemplating your action, you can avoid a lot of pain.

Now, if you've already wounded yourself, here are a few ideas that will move you toward healing:

Recognize the seriousness, sinfulness, or foolishness of what you've done.

Take full responsibility for your actions—no excuses or blame-casting.

Accept the consequences of your actions without anger, bitterness, or complaint.

Change your dangerous attitudes or behaviors immediately, if they are continuing.

Ask for God's forgiveness, knowing He is ready and willing to forgive as soon as you ask.

Forgive yourself, giving up your guilt, shame, and self-recrimination.

Make apologies and, if possible, restitution to any other casualties of your actions.

Learn from your past, so you become a stronger, better person.

Encourage others not to make the same mistakes you have.

Thank God that He can turn your self-wounds into something positive.

All of these healing measures can be summed in the words of Peter: "Now it's time to change your ways! Turn to face God so he can wipe away your sins, pour out showers of blessing to refresh you" (Acts 3:19, The Message). In the classic, *My Heart—Christ's Home,* Robert Boyd Munger uses the analogy of a house to describe how "room by room" we turn our hearts over to Christ. Munger says to imagine that one day Christ comes to your door and smells something dead inside. He looks you in the eye and declares that the offending object is in your closet. He asks if you will let Him clean it out. Munger then describes his own experience in this scenario: "With trembling fingers I passed the key to Him. He took it, walked over to the door, opened it, entered, took out all the putrefying stuff that was rotting there, and threw it away. Then He cleaned the closet and painted it. It was done in a moment's time. Oh, what victory and release to have that dead thing out of my life."

Nothing will erase your wounds, but God offers comfort and healing. For "there is no condemnation for those who belong to Christ Jesus" (Romans 8:1).

UNFAILING HOPE

Friendly fire and self-inflicted wounds represent two of the most grievous types of pain. The damage is done at close range and the echo of the blast can resound for years. Yet when I am laid low by those I trust or by my own foolishness, I know that I can go to God. I can go to Him...

- when friends have deserted me.
- when those I trust have turned against me.
- when loneliness is darker than night.
- when my poor choices have trapped me.
- when sin has served its consequences.
- when guilt and shame overpower me.

These are the desperate times when I've needed God the most. I don't always feel God's presence, but I know He's there. I might not see His hand, but it's always capably guiding me. I can't hear His voice, but it never ceases to broadcast the greatness of His love for me. This is what faith is all about.

So no matter what difficulty I encounter, I cling to those powerful words of Paul: "I am convinced that nothing can ever separate us from his love. Death can't, and life can't. The angels can't, and the demons can't. Our fears for today, our worries about tomorrow, and even the powers of hell can't keep God's love away" (Romans 8:38). When I read these words, I know there is always hope.

CHAPTER 11

TRIUMPH FROM TRAGEDY

LIFE ISN'T ALWAYS FAIR.

John Bunyan was thirty-two when he was arrested—for preaching at his own church!—and sent to Bradford Prison. The jailor promised to set the young man free if he would only stop preaching. But Bunyan insisted that he was doing nothing wrong, so for twelve years he sat in a cold, damp cell. During this time he kept a positive attitude and refused to let his circumstances get him down. He even wrote that God had turned his prison into a blessed place. Bunyan used his jail stint to encourage his fellow prisoners, pray, and write at least six books. He saw this adversity as a wonderful time to study the Bible and meditate on the spiritual aspects of life.

Finally, in 1672, he was set free and the whole city celebrated.

Three years later he was again arrested for preaching. All those who attended his church were discouraged. Except Bunyan, who accepted the turn of events as just another opportunity to read, meditate, and write. During the next six months in the cold, dark, depressing prison, Bunyan wrote his masterpiece—one of the best-selling books of all time: *The Pilgrim's Progress*.

Bunyan's greatest triumph was the result of his greatest tragedy. As George Meredeth wrote, "There is nothing the body suffers the soul may not profit by." God uses every battle to shape a man to become the best he can possibly be. In God's economy, nothing that happens is ever wasted. Og Mandino insists that one of the most important keys to success is to "search for the seed of good in every adversity."

In our culture of ease and comfort, we do all we can to avoid adversity. We think of hardship as some dreadful misfortune or terrible curse. We consider difficulties inconvenient at best, and catastrophic at worst.

In years past, people have viewed pain much more pragmatically. They believed difficulties to be an integral, unavoidable part of life. In fact, they saw troubles as something to be embraced. Nearly two thousand years ago, the apostle James told us to welcome our wounds as opportunities (see James 1:2–4).

Every adversity contains a lesson. Many lessons cannot be learned any other way. It's one of the great ironies of life that pain may be among God's richest gifts. Our trials and adversities hold powerful teachings, which render our sufferings not only positive and meaningful, but necessary.

God doesn't want any experience in our lives to go to waste. For this reason He makes sure that our wounds hold more benefits than most of us are ever aware. James Buckman wrote, "Every trial endured and weathered in the right spirit makes a soul nobler and stronger than it was before." Those who have not experienced any adversity risk a shallow, self-absorbed life, for it is through our difficulties that we experience the most growth. Let's look at six of the ways adversity can help us grow.

ADVERSITY DEVELOPS PATIENCE

Adversity slows us down. Sometimes it stops us dead in our tracks. In this quick-paced, move-as-fast-as-you-can world, we don't wait for anything. We race here and there, uncertain where we are going or what we want. Difficulties show us that we can't outrun life with its fears and disappointments and challenges. They force us to wait. To wait on time. To wait on others. To wait on God. They remind us that healing is usually a process, not merely the flip of a switch. And the more we pressure the process, the longer it takes.

Most of us are impatient. We like to see things happen quickly, and we get frustrated when the pace isn't as fast as we think it should be. We love to speed, but our wounds slam on the brakes. We can complain and stomp our feet. But what good does that do?

Troubles set their own pace. They demand patience. For when we move too quickly, we miss much—the colors, the details, sometimes even the essence of life. In a world where the accomplishment of a goal is emphasized more than the journey getting there, we skim and scan and skate as fast as we can, unaware of all that we have overshot. Speed handicaps our ability to concentrate and absorb. Patience allows us to learn incomparable lessons and gives us the time to weave those lessons into the fabric of our character.

We have no time for patience. Related words like *silence, stillness, contemplation, calmness, tranquillity,* and *endurance* seem to belong to a bygone era. Yet it is here that we find our true selves. It is here that we draw near to God.

ADVERSITY INCREASES MATURITY

John Patrick said, "Pain makes man think."

He might also have added that it helps us grow and mature. Wounds can give us depth and wisdom. We learn more from adversity than from prosperity. Prosperity may be attractive, but it adds no positive or long-lasting enhancements to our character. It allows us to become shallow and sheltered. Hard times and difficult circumstances, however, plunge us to the depths of life—discovering truth, solving problems, accepting limitations.

We live in a world where we do all we can to avoid difficulties, but this only traps us in our immaturity. Maturity faces its problems and heartaches head-on, doing all it can to work through them with a positive attitude. Even if they can't be solved quickly—or *ever*—walking through this process creates personal depth that no other experience can duplicate.

Maturity requires experience coping with the challenges of life. Someone once wrote, "A smooth sea never made a skillful mariner." This wise person knew that rough waters season our souls. When a mother bird pushes her babies from the nest, she creates an immediate crisis. Yet out of this crisis the babies learn to fly. Without this trauma the babies would stay in the nest and starve. Difficulties force us to face reality, stretch our wings, and see what possibilities may open up to us.

It is through our hard times that our maturity ripens and wisdom follows. The Greek poet Aeschylus wrote, "Pain that cannot forget falls upon the heart until, against our will, comes wisdom to us by the grace of God above." Wise people are those who have lived full lives, mining truth from every experience. They do not resent difficulties; they see them as a means to growth. They recognize that adversity keeps you sharp, opening doors of insight that would otherwise remain closed for a lifetime. They have discovered an amazing maxim of life—namely, that adversity provides wisdom, and wisdom lights the path for the best approach to adversity.

As Solomon wrote, "Happy is the person who finds wisdom and gains understanding. For the profit of wisdom is better than silver, and her wages are better than gold. She offers you life in her right hand, and riches and honor in her left" (Proverbs 3:13–16).

ADVERSITY TEACHES COMPASSION

When we have personally experienced the difficulties of life—fear, rejection, betrayal, shame, loneliness, hurt—we develop a gentle heart toward others in pain. Morrie Swartz said, "Now that I'm suffering, I feel closer to people who suffer than I ever did before.... I feel their anguish as if it were my own."

The eyes of the long-haul sufferer have been opened to life's world of hurts; he instantly recognizes pain in someone else's eyes. He hears it in their voice. Ignoring the quiet cries for help becomes harder, because he's been there, and he remembers the times when no one seemed to notice his suffering. Or if someone did notice, they didn't take time to reach out. Most crushing of all were those times when people reached out, only to judge him or give him trite, simplistic responses.

Compassion walks alongside, trying (and able) to understand another's heart. It exercises empathy and sensitivity. It willingly embraces those in pain and weeps with those who weep.

It's easy to become calloused and minimize suffering. Our hearts can so easily grow hard. But difficulties soften our hearts and make us less judgmental. Myla Kabal-Zinn learned this truth: "Each difficult moment has the potential to open my eyes and open my heart." Those who have felt pain, see the pain of others. As Jesus saw all the people gather about Him, Scripture tells us that He felt compassion, "because their problems were so great and they didn't know what to do or where to go" (Matthew 9:36, TLB).

Compassion has many faces. It is gentle. It is full of mercy and grace. It is love in action.

Eric never understood grief until his father was killed in a head-on collision by a drunk driver. Now he knows the emptiness of loss.

Dan impatiently told people, "If you can't change it, just get over it!" Then his wife left him and their two young boys for another woman. The sting of confusion, abandonment, and betrayal is something he will never forget.

Hard times changed Eric and Dan. Now they reach out more and give less advice. They show love and compassion. I see gentleness in their eyes, and I know that if someone were in pain, either one would immediately drop what he was doing and walk the difficult road with the needy one.

ADVERSITY STRENGTHENS COURAGE

Matt was shocked when, at age thirty-two, he was diagnosed with leukemia. He cried and prayed and grew very angry.

After a two-year battle, having now been declared symptom-free, Matt sat in my office.

"How has this changed you?" I asked.

He smiled. "First of all, I'm thankful for every day. Each moment of life is a wonderful gift. Second, I'm not as fearful.

Cancer gives you courage. You come to realize, *If I can face this, I can face anything.*"

We develop courage by surviving difficult times and by challenging adversity. Pain gives you courage. Suffering makes you brave. Trauma tests the mettle of man. When there are no battles, by definition there can be no courage.

Courage is the ability to withstand hardship—the willingness to look fear in the eye and stand firm. Pain and danger mold a heart of valor. The wounded man naturally wants to withdraw and retreat. The world no longer seems safe or trustworthy, and even the simplest activities loom before him as feats demanding great nerve.

A man who faces his difficulties without caving in develops a courage that impacts the way he thinks and feels and acts. Life is elastic—it either expands to become a giant or shrinks down to its true proportions, depending upon the way we deal with adversity. It's our courage that shapes our character.

ADVERSITY BUILDS CHARACTER

Character is the commitment to doing what is true, right, good, and wise, regardless of the cost. In a season of struggle, we find ourselves tempted to take the easiest path, rather than the right path. Wounds tempt us to compromise. We justify questionable actions and convince ourselves that they are acceptable "under certain conditions."

Adversity tests who we are; it either strengthens us or weakens us. It shows our character.

A teenaged boy responded to a "Help Wanted" sign in a local store window. The owner sent the boy up to the attic—which was dirty, hot, and cramped—to sort several boxes of paperwork. It was a miserable job. At the bottom of the last box, the boy found a ten-dollar bill. When he had finished, he took the money to the owner.

"You passed the test," the owner said. "You completed a hard job without complaint and you showed honesty. I want someone with that sort of character to work for me."

Personally, I have never encountered a difficulty that didn't make me stronger in some way. And when the pain was at its peak intensity—that was when I grew most.

Character is rarely developed when all goes well. Suffering strengthens one's soul, clarifies one's vision, and raises one's character above the ordinary. As I've studied the greatest men and women of history, it's amazing how many of them experienced severe adversity. In fact, it appears that the very qualities that made them great were forged in the darkest days of their lives.

ADVERSITY DEEPENS FAITH

Hard times and deep wounds remind us of our humanity, our humility, and our utter dependence upon God. Adversity reminds us that we're not nearly as self-sufficient as we'd like to think ourselves. It beckons us to faith. Pope John Paul II said, "Faith leads us beyond ourselves. It leads us directly to God." I frequently wonder how people can handle difficulties without God. Helen Keller learned through her blindness and deafness that "a simple childhood faith...solves all the problems that come to us."

Our wounds drive us closer to God. They force us to our knees as we cry out to Him. Martin Luther wrote that "except under troubles, trials, and vexations, prayer cannot rightly be made."

It's true, isn't it? When everything is sunshine and smooth sailing, our prayers lose their passion. Ah, but when the darkness falls, when the disappointment comes, when fear descends, that's when we pray with all our hearts.

Maybe the old saying is right: "Need teaches us to pray." Desperation improves our perspective and deepens our dependence. Helmut Thielicke wrote that "we learn to pray best in suffering." Why? Because it leads us back to the strong arms of God, where we discover all the peace and rest for which we so deeply yearn. Jesus invites us: "Come to me, all of you who are weary and carry heavy burdens, and I will give you rest" (Matthew 11:28).

When all is well, we forget how badly we need God. When difficulties grab hold of us and pull us down, we definitely know we need Him. George Mueller emphasized this when he wrote, "The only way to learn strong faith is to endure strong trials."

What, then, is the greatest enemy to our faith? *It's pros-perity.* When everything comes easy for us, we grow lazy, proud, and selfish. When troubles don't broaden us, our world shrinks to those issues immediately before our noses. Jean De La Bruyere wrote, "Out of difficulties, grow miracles."

Without faith, miracles lay unclaimed.

Without difficulty, no need for faith is apparent.

In the end, then, it is our wounds that provide wings that catch the currents of faith...and carry us to higher vistas than we would have otherwise known. As A. W. Tozer writes, "It is doubtful whether God can bless a man greatly until he has hurt him deeply."

GOD IS GOOD

Celebrate your wounds, for they make you so much better. James Emery White says it well:

> If there is any tenderness to my heart, it has come through its being broken.
>
> If anything of worth flows through my soul, it flows out of a desert.
>
> If there is any trustworthiness to my mind, it was forged on the anvil of doubt.
>
> If my actions seem vigorous, they originated in blindness and frailty.

If there is depth to any of my relationships, it has come through wounding.

Let's stop bemoaning our pain and feeling sorry for ourselves. For no matter how difficult our struggles or how deep our wounds, they carry with them great lessons. They teach us much about ourselves, life, and God. They enrich us in ways that nothing else can. They give us the patience to endure, the maturity to grow, the compassion to reach out to others in need, the courage to survive, the character to transform something terribly hurtful into something positive, and the faith to know that we are not alone.

We may indeed go through seasons of suffering. In fact, we can count on them. Jesus said, "In this godless world you will continue to experience difficulties. But take heart! I've conquered the world" (John 16:33, The Message). For some, that season of hardship and heartache will be longer, for others, shorter. But all suffering has its end. God promises, "He will restore, support, and strengthen you, and he will place you on a firm foundation" (1 Peter 5:10).

Make no mistake: Triumph is best born out of tragedy.

CHAPTER 12

RECOVERY AND RECUPERATION

TROY WAS ON THE VERGE OF BURNOUT.

He worked twelve hours a day, six days a week. In his time off he remodeled his house, taught Sunday School, and took college classes on-line. Troy seemed to race through life at full speed, never slowing down. He had taken no vacations for six years, and he probably hadn't laughed in seven. The pressures of life wore him out; he hardly had time to breathe. Troy's spiritual life had once been strong, but now God seemed as far away as Troy's peace of mind.

When we have been wounded, we need rest. In order to get back on our feet, we have to plan intentional interludes. We have to stop in our tracks and catch our breath. In an out-of-control world, recovery does not come easy. When we get hit, we have to get out of the fracas so our wounds can be properly cleaned and bandaged. We guys often have trouble extracting ourselves from the battle; we like to stay in the thick of it. But as Chuck Swindoll writes, "Renewal and restoration are not luxuries. They are essentials. There is absolutely nothing enviable or spiritual about a nervous breakdown, nor is an ultra-busy schedule the mark of a productive life." So in order to move toward recovery and recuperation, we need to slow down. We need to spiritually surrender. And we need to sleep.

SLOW DOWN

Life is busy.

Work is busy.

Family is busy.

I might complain at how fast-paced everything is, but I must confess that I'm the one who has trouble slowing down. I like to pack my schedule as tight as possible. If I have any free time at all, even if it's just five minutes, I look for ways to fill it. I love speed. The faster, the better. The more I can accomplish, the happier I am. The adrenaline rush makes me feel alive, even if it does wear me out. If there is nothing to do or nowhere to go, I feel lost.

When we slow down, we are able to stop the *doing* and just *be*. Our culture frequently defines us by our actions; what we do is who we are. But God looks deeper. He says that who we are depends on our heart. Yet we are frequently too busy to get to know our own heart.

Healing is also hard to come by unless we slow down. When our body is not well, it seems to know that taking it easy is the only way to get better. Yet when we are wounded in nonphysical ways, we keep moving as if nothing were wrong.

Oh, we feel the pain, but we don't slacken our pace. And that's why we don't recover nearly as fast as we could. When wounded, we must slow down, whether we want to or not.

Now there are slowdowns, and there are slowdowns. The most effective season of rest is one that is characterized by five important qualities:

Silence

We are surrounded by noise—way too much noise. All this commotion can easily increase your stress, anger, and impatience. So turn off the television, radio, and stereo. Give yourself an audio fast; listen to the quiet. It's amazing what you can hear in the silence: wind, rain, birds. Silence takes us back to the basics. We mine peace from the quarry of quiet.

Noise distracts us. It keeps us from thinking and feeling. Sometimes noise, even the noise of our own voice, keeps us from hearing what we need in order to heal our wounds and live life to its fullest. A. W. Tozer writes, "More spiritual progress can be made in one short moment of speechless silence in the presence of God than in years of mere study." Decibels are disruptive. Volume keeps us from healing. Too many words can also block the healing process. But when all is quiet and we settle into the holiness of silence, then and only then can we hear God's still, small voice, His gentle whisper. Noise can deafen us, but quietude prepares our hearts and opens our ears. Those are the conditions that allow healing to begin.

Simplicity

The older we get, the more complex things appear. I frequently scratch my head and wonder, *How did life get so complicated?*

We long for the joy and peace of simplicity. Someone once said, "Simplicity is the dream of all who do too much." And we all probably do too much.

Simplicity eases our stress, calms our spirit, and cleans away our clutter. Hans Hoffman wrote, "The ability to simplify means to eliminate the unnecessary so that the necessary may speak." When our days are filled with unnecessary clutter, we trip and fall and feel claustrophobic. It's hard to heal when life is cluttered. Many are the types of clutter that can steal our simplicity:

- *Physical* clutter consists of all the stuff you can see and touch, which fills our living space. We collect stuff because it gives us a false sense of security, comfort, and pride. But that's deceptive. In reality, physical clutter creates disorder, stress, and more work.
- *Mental* clutter involves an overload of ideas and images, issues to consider, quandaries to puzzle over, threats to worry about. You literally have *too much on your mind,* and this mental clutter can lead to distractions, obsessions, or impure thoughts.
- *Emotional* clutter consists mostly of unprocessed, unresolved, and sometimes unrecognized feelings—

fears, insecurities, anger, anxiety. When your life is full of emotional clutter, you probably feel confused and anxious much of the time. Anger may flare unexpectedly. You have a sense of being on the edge or out of control.

- *Spiritual* clutter has mostly to do with unrecognized and unconfessed sin in your life. Attitudes of defiance, greed, dishonesty, anger, jealousy, bitterness, lack of love, pride, lust, or selfish ambition may crowd your heart—especially if you haven't kept current with God. As we clear our clutter, simplicity opens the door to healing.

Stillness

We can't heal unless we stop, determine the nature of our wound, rest, and regroup. But we tend to encounter least resistance along the path of perpetual motion; we can always find something to do or somewhere to go. Life grows so hectic that we are always on the run. We miss the joys of life, and we frequently miss God. No wonder He tells us firmly, "Be still, and know that I am God" (Psalm 46:10, NIV). The Lord is assuring us that it's not all on our shoulders. If we stop, the world will not fall apart. He is telling us to slow down and reflect on:

- who God is.
- what He has done for us.
- His wonderful works in creation.

- His plans and promises.
- His amazing love.

As we reflect on things like these, God's peace fills us, and life takes on a different meaning.

Most of us pack our schedules with no margins, no space for stillness or reflection. At this pace it becomes difficult, if not impossible, to discover and appreciate all the things in life that really matter. As we race to reach our goals and obligations, or just to keep up, peace becomes a nice idea and nothing more. The faster we go, the more we tend to skim the surface of our life instead of going deep. We do what is quick and expedient, not necessarily what is important. We listen in sound bites, grab meals on the run, exercise when we can fit it in, and produce only what is demanded. We say yes to whatever pressures us and urges us faster, leaving no time to nurture those things we truly value.

Such a lifestyle fills time without filling us as persons. It leaves us relationally, emotionally, and spiritually superficial. Being still slows us down, giving us the time to grow deep and to enjoy life. I love the words of King David when he wrote, "He leadeth me beside the still waters. He restoreth my soul" (Psalm 23:2–3, KJV). That's where I want to spend as much time as possible—beside the still waters.

Solitude

Sometimes people stress me and wear me out. I enjoy people, but sometimes I just want to escape the demands and expectations, even when they are reasonable. As guys, we sometimes need to hide in our garage or go fishing or play golf or hike in the woods. In these ways we escape and seek out solitude. We all need our refuge, our sanctuary, our oasis. Even Jesus needed a break; at different times He'd escape to the desert, the mountains, the olive groves, or the remote side of the lake. After the murder of His cousin, He needed some space, "because so many people were coming and going." Jesus said to his disciples, "'Come with me by yourselves to a quiet place and get some rest.' So they went away by themselves in a boat to a solitary place" (Mark 6:31–32, NIV).

We all need moments and places of solitude. In solitude we can think and pray. We can get in touch with our true feelings and sort out our uninhibited thoughts. Brennan Manning reminds us that we all have "a compulsive desire to present a perfect image to the public so that everybody will admire us and nobody will know us." In solitude you can be the real you with no one to please or impress. In solitude you can be completely honest. There is a beauty and freedom in solitude, but its purpose isn't to isolate us. Solitude prepares us to be more loving and compassionate when we return to the crowds. Solitude makes us better persons—better husbands, fathers, friends, and neighbors. Solitude is a place where:

- truth is pondered.
- meaning is found.

- wrongs are forgiven.
- visions are cast.
- character is developed.
- love is nurtured.
- faith is deepened.
- healing is discovered.

Solitude fills up our tank, so we can return to the battle energized and raring to go.

Savor

Life is full of wonder and delight. Every day we are surrounded by beauty and goodness and miracles. Yet we are so busy and hectic that we rarely see the glories all around us. When we are wounded, it is even harder to see that which is bright and positive. Our troubles and pain can blind us, but the goodness of life is healing. If we can savor the best parts of life—enjoy, delight, appreciate them—then our days become an adventure. Celebrate all that surrounds you. Slow down and have fun.

Savoring life involves discovering all that God meant it to be. David wrote that "the heavens tell of the glory of God. The skies display his marvelous craftsmanship" (Psalm 19:1). But it's not just the heavens that show God's glory; it's everything we see, hear, feel, taste, and smell. The world is full of wonder. So soak it in and savor it. Smile and laugh and love. Here are some ways to savor life:

Watch a sunrise.

Sing or whistle.

Lie on your back and look at the stars.

Reread a good book.

Listen to your favorite music.

Laugh a lot.

Walk through the woods.

Spend time with friends.

Play with children.

Count your blessings.

Slowing down can make all the difference in the world. It brings joy and peace. It also opens your heart and mind to the Maker of the universe—the One who loves you and is waiting to heal your deepest wounds.

SPIRITUAL SURRENDER

This is a spiritual universe. Its most obvious challenges may be physical, but its best solutions are spiritual—coming directly or indirectly from the strong and gentle hand of God. When adversity comes, let it drive you and keep you close to God. To walk through troubles and trials believing we are alone is tragic.

Pain has a way of blunting our awareness of God's closeness—at the very moment we need that awareness most. Yet God is always with us, whether we are aware of it or not. He knows that pain serves a constructive purpose in our lives, so He doesn't protect us from it. Rather, He walks through it with us and fills it with His presence. God's peace and power comes alive as we abide in the depths of our pain. His infinite resources, once theoretical, now become real. But we must choose to let them become realized in our experience. We have to stop fighting God. We have to surrender.

Listen to Him

Every day, in a thousand different ways God tries to communicate with us. He wants to guide us toward good and direct us away from evil. He wants to teach, comfort, direct, warn, encourage, and enlighten us. But we are so preoccupied with the physical realm—what we see, taste, touch, smell, and hear—that we miss the message God is sending. God wants to break through to us, but He is waiting for us to be ready. He is waiting for us to listen.

God speaks to us in every way imaginable. He speaks through creation, thoughts, feelings, people, music, Scripture, miracles, coincidences, peace, passion, creativity, and even our pain. God will use anything to get our attention and make us aware of Him. God even makes this bold promise to us: "If you look for me in earnest, you will find me when you seek me. I will be found by you..." (Jeremiah 29:13–14).

So let us look and listen for Him. And when we listen, let us do so...

- **Patiently:** Know that God speaks when and how He wishes. He is not bound by our timetable. As a friend of mine says, "God is rarely early, but He is never late."

- **Expectantly:** We can be confident that God will speak to us in one way or another. He is not silent. He is not distant.
- **Carefully:** We must actively pay attention. The noise of this world is sometimes so loud that it drowns out God. We must also be careful that we don't confuse our desires with God's voice.
- **Excitedly:** God has great things in store for us. He yearns to speak wisdom, joy, encouragement, and peace into our life. He has amazing, wonderful things in store for us if we will only listen.

The more we listen, the more we will hear. God says, "Listen, and I will tell you where to get food that is good for the soul! Come to me with your ears wide open. Listen, for the life of your soul is at stake" (Isaiah 55:2–3). We can listen anytime, and in any place, for God is with us twenty-four hours a day, eagerly waiting to be heard.

Talk to Him

Everything about God is relational. He never ceases to reach out and speak to us. Prayer is our opportunity to reach out and speak to Him. Prayer is no magic formula; it is merely opening up our thoughts and feelings and needs to the great Comforter. When I'm feeling most broken, I want to run away from my pain. These are the times I need to cry out to my heavenly Father. Malcolm Muggeridge reminds us, "The Comforter needs only to be summoned. The need is the call, the call is the presence, and the presence is the Comforter, the Spirit of Truth."

Prayer reminds us that we are weak and need someone who is strong. We may not want to admit our weakness and need when all is well, but when the suffering is great we can no longer deny it. So when we hit bottom, we cry out for wisdom, strength, and healing. My friend John Van Diest tells me that in response to prayer, God provides:

- **Protection:** He is our refuge and shelter in the time of storm. If God is with us, who can stand against us?
- **Power:** He has infinite strength and with Him all things are possible. He holds the universe together and nothing is too hard for Him.
- **Provision:** He can and will meet our every need. Yet only He knows our true needs; frequently we confuse wants with needs.
- **Peace:** He is the Prince of Peace and the source of all peace. When life is chaotic, He calms the most troubled heart.
- **Perspective:** He can guide and direct our ways when we get lost in anger, fear, or confusion. He is the light when all is dark.
- **Passion:** He can bring joy and excitement back into our life when pain has sucked us dry. He can give us an abundant life.

So talk to God continually—in the morning and at night, in crisis and when all is well. Go to Him honestly and humbly. He is waiting to bless you in ways that will strengthen and deepen you. All you have to do is ask with a pure and selfless faith. Maybe healing has never come because you never asked.

Yield to Him

Yielding to God involves letting God have control and placing your life in His capable hands. It is recognizing that as Pam Vredevelt writes, God "is on a mission to revive, refresh and resurrect the dead places in our soul." This is not necessarily a painless process, but it will leave you a better person. "'If you return to me, I will restore you…. I will give you back your health and heal your wounds,' says the LORD" (Jeremiah 15:19; 30:17).

Yielding involves step-by-step, minute-by-minute progress in God's direction. James writes, "Draw close to God, and God will draw close to you" (James 4:8). This is not a hard thing! It just means swallowing your pride, admitting you need some help, and letting Him help you. This is a lopsided deal. You have nothing to lose and everything to gain. God is faithful even when you are engulfed in troubles, trials, or tragedy. In these situations…

YOU SAY	GOD SAYS
"It's impossible."	"All things are possible."
"I'm tired."	"I will give you rest."
"I can't go on."	"My grace is sufficient."
"I'm lost."	"I will direct your steps."

"I'm not able."	"I am able."
"I can't do it."	"I will supply all your needs."
"I'm afraid."	"Fear not."
"I'm worried."	"Cast all your cares on Me."

Maybe you've noticed, God has a faithful answer to each of our struggles. As we follow Him, He leads us into a healing grace. The closer we get to Him, the healthier we get. Catherine Marshall writes, "The strengthening of faith comes through staying with it in the hour of trial."

Life loses its luster when we lose sight of God. It grows dark and cold and cruel. Yet when we surrender to Him, we find a wider, deeper eternal picture. God gives life meaning.

- When you CRY, He will COMFORT you.
- When you are HAPPY, He will LAUGH with you.
- When you need to TALK, He will LISTEN.
- When you need DIRECTION, He will GUIDE.
- When you are LONELY, He will be PRESENT.
- When you are FRIGHTENED, He will PROTECT you.
- When you need a FRIEND, He will CARE for you.
- When you need HOPE, He will NEVER let you down.

We get all this. And all we have to do is surrender.

SLEEP

Chuck was having trouble making decisions. He was also impatient, negative, and easily ticked off. At work he struggled with concentration, and at home nothing seemed to make him happy. "So what's wrong with me?" he asked.

"Tell me how you sleep," I said.

"I don't need much sleep," Chuck said. "I stay up till about two and usually fall asleep in my easy chair. Then I wake up about five in the morning. I'm a little groggy at first, but after three or four cups of coffee I'm ready to go."

"I think your problem is lack of sleep," I said.

"But sleep feels like a waste of time," he said. "I've got so much to do that I can't afford to sleep more."

"If you keep up this pattern, your symptoms will get a lot worse."

Chuck didn't take me seriously, but his wife did. She insisted that he go to the beach alone for a long weekend and get some real sleep. That night he fell asleep at 7 p.m. And didn't wake up until 1 p.m. the following afternoon. He got up, ate, walked the beach, and fell asleep at 4 p.m. The next morning he got up at 8 a.m., feeling like a new person—more energetic, positive, and excited about life than he had felt in years. When he returned home, many of his symptoms had gone away.

There is incredible power in sound sleep. In fact, you cannot function properly or recover from wounds without solid sleep. When we experience stressful challenges, our bodies demand more sleep. If we feel beat up, burned out, or broken in any way, sleep is an important component of recovery.

Much of our physical and emotional healing is helped by a good night's sleep. Trouble will only ensue without it.

Yet researchers estimate that two-thirds of Americans don't get the sleep they truly need. In this society, where you are respected and rewarded for your output, it can just be too tempting to stay up late to finish one more task, then get up early for a good start on the day. The trouble is, you'll usually pay for that decision in weariness and stress.

Our fast-paced, get-more-done, twenty-four-hour lifestyle seems to see sleep as optional. But nothing could be further from the truth. People tend to brag about their ability to "get by" on very few hours of slumber, but if you've convinced yourself that you do just fine on four or five hours a night (and sometimes less), think again. Studies have found that sleep-deprived people are more prone to depression and health problems, including diabetes. They are more likely to lose control emotionally and significantly more likely to have accidents. Sleep is one of the primary ways the body and mind renew themselves. Consistent, sound sleep energizes our attitude, reduces emotional turmoil, and empowers us to manage life's stress.

Your body and mind can function only so long without sufficient restful sleep. How can you ensure you're getting enough? Your answers to the following three questions can help point you in the right direction and protect you from exhaustion, stress, and burnout.

How much do you sleep?

Sleep is one of your most important daily physical needs—more important than food and exercise. Food is critical, but you could survive for thirty to fifty days without it. Exercise is also valuable, but people do manage to live for years without much of it. If you go longer than thirty-six hours without sleep, however, you will lose your concentration and become emotionally unstable.

Sleep energizes your body, calms your anxieties, refreshes your attitude, and increases your creativity. Arranging your schedule to get at least seven hours each night is one of the best ways to combat weariness. You can't afford to cheat on sleep. Going without it will hurt you more than you think. You deserve your rest. More importantly, you can't function without it.

You were not designed to function for extended periods without rest. If your activities are keeping you from getting the sleep you need, reconsider what you have squeezed into your days. This might be the time to sort out your priorities and cross a few things off your to-do list. If your sleep deprivation becomes chronic, your body and spirit will pay the price. And the irony is that when you "miss out" on some activities by getting a good night's slumber, you can usually make them up another day in addition to your usual schedule of tasks, because of your improved efficiency and concentration.

How well do you sleep?

If you've ever spent a night tossing or turning or waking up every few hours, you know that *how well* you sleep is just as important as *how long* you sleep. When you don't wake up refreshed, it's usually the result of disruptive noises, physical discomfort, medical issues, or worries.

Whatever the problem, if you wake in the middle of the night and can't fall back to sleep in less than fifteen minutes, you must do something. The longer you lie awake, the more frustrated you're likely to be, and this in turn can make it even harder to sleep. Many people have found the following strategies helpful for coping with middle-of-the-night wakefulness:

- Get out of bed, but keep the lights low. (Bright lights tend to stimulate wakefulness.)
- Have a cup of noncaffeinated tea, hot water with lemon, or warm milk.
- Read a relaxing book or a calming, reassuring passage from your Bible.
- If problems and worries have been keeping you awake, write them down in a journal.
- Pray for any friends or family members who come to mind.
- After fifteen minutes, go back to bed.

Most of the time, one or more of these ideas will help you fall back to sleep. If they don't, get up and repeat the process, but this time stay up for a half-hour. If you have tried these and are still tossing and turning after more than three nights in a row, talk to your doctor about further remedies.

How do you prepare for sleep?

What you do when you're awake—especially in the evening— can significantly affect how long and how well you sleep. That's because your mind tends to continue processing whatever is on your mind as you prepare for bed. If you were mentally working on a problem, you continue trying to solve it. If you were wrestling with a fear, you continue worrying about it.

Sometimes getting to sleep seems impossible. You lie in bed—worn out, exhausted, yearning for rest—but your mind is racing a hundred miles an hour. You check the clock every ten minutes, count sheep until you go crazy, and review your schedule for the next day. And the longer you can't sleep, the more frustrated you get. The greater the frustration, the more adrenaline is pumped through your body, pushing your precious slumber even further away.

Lingering anger, frustration, and conflicts can either prevent sleep or make slumber uneasy and restless. You can improve your sleep dramatically by resolving such difficulties two or three hours before placing your head on the pillow— or at least making a specific plan to resolve them the next day. The reality is that high stress causes insomnia, and insomnia in turn causes increased stress.

Similarly, try not to spend the hours before bedtime solving complicated problems, processing painful memories, or facing fears. These are best done with trusted friends during the day. The evening is the time to slow down the body and brain. Rehearsing difficulties does the opposite, rousing your brain instead of relaxing it. If you can't complete these tasks during the day or in the early evening, intentionally put them on hold until the next day. Here are a few ideas to try one hour before bedtime:

Avoid caffeinated drinks.

Turn off TV news or tense dramas.

Listen to relaxing music.

Avoid vigorous exercise.

Read something positive.

Stop working on energizing projects.

Put on comfortable clothing.

Dim the lights.

Spend time in prayer.

Whether it's before going to sleep or upon awakening in the middle of the night, prayer can help calm your spirit and relax your body. There is something soothing and comforting about knowing that God understands your every challenge and struggle. By reminding yourself that God is in control, you can truly let go, and as Solomon says, "Your sleep will be sweet" (Proverbs 3:24, NIV).

Elijah was a busy man, but he soon learned that we all have our limits. Within a short time span he encouraged a hundred courageous leaders and confronted King Ahab of Israel.

He challenged 850 evil prophets to a contest and won. Then he ran an uphill marathon to the capital city, only to discover that Queen Jezebel had ordered him captured and killed within twenty-four hours. He escaped the city, fled over a hundred miles to the south, and then hiked deep into an unforgiving desert. That was where Elijah collapsed.

He had had enough and could go no further. Elijah was burned out, exhausted, lonely, and utterly discouraged. His emotional wounds went deep, and he could see no hope. "I have had enough, LORD," he said. "Take my life" (1 Kings 19:4).

Anyone who pushes too hard will sooner or later hit a wall. God knew that Elijah needed a chance for recovery and recuperation. Sometimes guys are stubborn. Sometimes we have to hit bottom before we are willing to look up. God let Elijah sleep—a long, deep, peaceful sleep. Then an angel woke him and gave him healthy food and fresh water. Elijah ate, drank, and slept some more. Once he had regained his strength, Elijah went on a forty-day journey of spiritual renewal to get to know God at a deeper, more real level than ever before.

Elijah emerged from this experience a stronger, healthier person. He also learned that if we don't slow down, spiritually surrender, and sleep, we risk being crushed by the challenges of life.

CHAPTER 13
TRUSTING AGAIN

"I GIVE UP! Why would I be stupid enough to ever trust anybody again?"

Kyle had just discovered that Lisa, his wife of seven years, had left him and their two children for another man—Kyle's best friend. The hurt pierced him like a bullet. Kyle loved Lisa with all his heart and thought they'd had a great relationship. But he'd missed the signs. For the past four years—more than half their marriage—Lisa had been secretly having an affair with Derek. During this same time, Kyle and Derek met for poker every Saturday night, went fishing together, and shared their dreams.

Kyle wanted to die.

Literally. Immediately.

If it hadn't been for their two small children, he might have ended it all. Sometimes a wound seems so deep that we think we can never recover from it.

In fact, we don't even want to try.

Deep wounds cause us to recoil and retreat. We withdraw and hide. We promise ourselves that we will never, never let anybody hurt us like that again. We put up strong defenses and build thick walls to guard our hearts from the cold winds and harsh cruelties of life. Our goal becomes self-protection, because we honestly doubt that we can survive another wound.

But the very strategies we employ to avoid harm become traps in themselves—snares with iron jaws that clamp down and hold us in our pain. We become so focused on our fear of more pain that we can't heal. We get stuck in a place that seems safe, but blocks us from any real growth.

Trusting again is hard. It involves putting ourselves in a situation where we might be hurt once more. And most of us find this too uncomfortable—or frightening. Our self-protection mechanism serves us well when it keeps us from foolishly offering our trust to someone we know is untrustworthy. But to refuse to trust at all because someone *may* be untrustworthy is equally foolish.

To grow, we must be intentional. Passivity means remaining stuck in our pain. But to actively step out, regardless of our fears, can open up opportunities that will make us healthier people. As we work our way back toward trusting again, we must willingly, intentionally make the following four crucial choices.

CHOICE #1: ACCEPT REALITY

Reality isn't always pretty, but it's better than the alternative. Reality is life; it's where we have to live. Acceptance looks unblinkingly at our situation and admits that *this is really how things are at the present moment.*

It may not be the way we wish it was.

It may not be what it might have been.

It may not be anything that seems right or logical or fair.

Even so, acceptance says, "This is what *is*. This is what I must deal with."

Someone once said, "Pain plants the flag of reality in the fortress of a rebel heart." Most of us guys have rebel hearts, and pain pays us the favor of a much-needed wake-up call.

Refusing either to exaggerate or to minimize, acceptance simply says, "This is reality. So, given that, what does God want me to do with it? And what resources will He provide for me, to help me do His will?"

Acceptance is the first step to healing. It allows us to evaluate the situation and determine what we might do next. Without acceptance we cannot develop a plan that moves us forward. We get stuck orbiting the pain and wondering why. As Virginia Satir writes, "Life is not the way it's supposed to be. It's the way it is. The way you cope with it is what makes the difference."

Reality may be harsh. It may throw us punches we never thought we could handle. But with God's help we can deal with more than we ever thought possible. Acceptance is a conscious choice that becomes the foundation on which we build the rest of our lives.

At seventeen, Joni broke her neck while diving from a floating dock into Chesapeake Bay. Suddenly, irreversibly, her world changed. Instead of an active, athletic, independent girl, she was a quadriplegic sentenced to spend the rest of her life in a wheelchair. This was a reality Joni desperately did not want to face, let alone accept. She prayed for healing, for a miracle, for anything to stop this nightmare.

One winter afternoon Joni looked out a window at her parent's home to see her sisters trotting their horses through the snow. Sadness overwhelmed her; she wished she could jump out of her wheelchair and onto a horse to join them. Later that day, Joni wheeled her chair outside to listen to the wind whistle through the pines and feel the soft snowflakes melt on her face.

"No, I couldn't ride horseback in the snow," she wrote, "but I could appreciate the pleasure of a snowy evening even while sitting still. Accepting my wheelchair didn't happen right then and there. That snowy evening was just one in a long series of many days when the Holy Spirit covered my hurt with His gentle grace."

As Joni Eareckson (now Tada) accepted her reality, she learned to draw by holding a pencil in her mouth. Soon she became a respected artist. As the years passed, she also became a bestselling author and a well-known speaker who has addressed large crowds in thirty-seven countries. Joni is also the founder and president of Joni and Friends, an organization that promotes Christian ministry in the disabled community worldwide. None of this would have happened if Joni had not first accepted her disability.

Acceptance is not sitting back passively to see what happens next. It does not stare at its wound, feeling sorry for itself. It does not stall out in the illusory worlds of If Only or What Might Have Been. Acceptance does not give up. It does not cry out to God, "I don't deserve this." Acceptance says, "I don't like this, but I know God can give me the strength to make it through."

Acceptance knows that while wounds may be uncomfortable or difficult to bear for the moment, they may also deliver powerful lessons. Keri West sums it up well when she writes that acceptance "works within today's reality while stretching toward tomorrow's possibility."

And one more thing. When you think about the reality of what *is*, you must reckon with the ultimate reality of a compassionate, loving, all-powerful God who inhabits this very instant in time. He is the Greater Reality above all other realities. It is in Him that "we live and move and have our being" (Acts 17:28, NIV). And though He may not choose to change your circumstances—just as He declined to grant Joni the healing for which she pleaded—He is still God Almighty. *Nothing* is too difficult for Him. You can do all things through Christ who strengthens you (see Philippians 4:13).

CHOICE #2: LET GO

Once we accept the reality of our wounds, we must learn to let go. Many of our wounds involve losses—something we had that has been taken away. Maybe we've lost a loved one, a friendship, a cherished hope, a dream. Maybe we've lost our health, our security, our reputation. It's easy to dwell on "the good old days." We all want to hold on to the happier memories of seasons gone by. But this keeps us trapped in the past and (let's face it) a reality which no longer exists. Therefore, to grow we need the courage to let go of burdens such as:

unhealthy relationships

negativity

anger

criticism

guilt and shame

self-pity

unrealistic expectations

need to be right

resentments

pride.

Isaiah says to "forget the former things; do not dwell on the past" (Isaiah 43:18, NIV). The past is unchangeable. M. Scott Peck writes that contentment is "being at peace with unchangeable circumstances, choices and mistakes of your past." Letting go moves us forward.

Once we let go of the past, we can let go of the negative emotions associated with the past—the anger, hurt, disappointment, bitterness, sorrow, fear, shame, regret. These negative emotions are a heavy load for anyone to carry. Too heavy. They weigh us down and darken our spirits. The tighter we cling to them, the more miserable we feel. These feelings become chains that keep us from growth. We drive through life with our eyes so focused on the rearview mirror, that we can't see the road in front of us.

Nobody said that letting go was easy!

Ben's fiancé, Jenny, was killed by a drunk driver on the way to their wedding. They had been high school sweethearts, and everyone considered them the perfect couple. Suddenly at twenty-three, she was dead, and he was devastated beyond words.

Some twenty years have passed since that dark day, and Ben is one of the nicest, brightest, most compassionate people I know. Yet he has never gone out on a date. Oh, he has plenty of women friends who would love to spend time with him, but he has never asked any of them out.

Ben is still in love with Jenny. Her picture still occupies a central place on the fireplace mantle of his small house, and her engagement ring remains in a wooden box on his desk. Until Ben can let go of Jenny, he will never be wholly happy.

CHOICE #3: TAKE RISKS

Life is a risk. Anything really worthwhile requires a risk. We risk being hurt again, we risk embarrassment, we risk losing what we have. Risks are as much a part of living as oxygen is part of the atmosphere. Every day delivers a fresh supply of risks to our doorstep.

In the wake of a wounding experience, however, we seek to avoid risks. We want to run away and build strong, impenetrable walls where no one and nothing can get to us.

We don't want to face the storms of life.

We don't want to deal with any more pressure or trauma.

We don't want to be afraid again, or grieved again, or disappointed again.

So brick by brick we build our walls and refuse to go anywhere or do anything or expose ourselves in any way.

We might call this kind of existence "safety and security."

In reality it's a living death.

Without risk we can neither grow nor improve. We become stale and stagnant. Avoiding risk puts us in a new kind of danger—danger of living a life of regret for what might have been. Geena Davis says, "If you risk nothing then you risk everything."

Risk takes courage. It takes stepping out into the scary unknown. Risk involves facing our fears and counting on the fact that a loving God remains in control of the details of our lives. David prayed, "I trust in you, O LORD; I say, 'You are my God.' My times are in your hands" (Psalm 31:14–15, NIV). The apostle Paul wrote, "If God is for us, who can ever be against us?" (Romans 8:31).

There is no real risk with God at our side. Moses gave instructions to the people of Israel that before any battle the priests were to stand before the warriors and say, "Do not be afraid as you go out to fight today! Do not lose heart or panic. For the LORD your God is going with you" (Deuteronomy 20:3–4).

Years ago I heard a saying that I repeat to myself whenever fear gets a hold on me: "Fear paralyzes faith, but faith paralyzes fear." If we keep our eyes focused on the object of faith, our faith grows. The apostle Peter discovered the truth of this when Jesus called him to walk across the churning surface of the sea one wild, black night. As long as Peter kept his eyes on Jesus, he could do the impossible. But as soon as he looked at the waves, he sank.

Fear tells us that we can't do it. Faith tells us that with God all things are possible. Phillip Yancey writes that faith "involves learning to trust that, out beyond the perimeter of fog, God still reigns and has not abandoned us, no matter how it may appear."

Risk means reaching out in spite of our fears. Florence Nightingale wrote, "How very little can be done under the spirit of fear." But with faith amazing things can happen. With faith we have the courage to risk. And those risks open the doors to tremendous rewards. I agree with Leo Buscaglia: "The person who risks nothing...may avoid suffering and sorrow, but he simply cannot learn and feel and change and grow and love and live."

Taking risks is crucial to moving beyond your wounds; it's the only way to use your pain as a springboard to a deeper faith. Risk holds onto faith and lets loose of fear; it means trusting that God has our best interest in mind. It's knowing that whatever happens, He will be our rock and refuge. Jeremiah said it well: "Blessed are those who trust in the LORD and have made the LORD their hope and confidence. They are like trees planted along a riverbank, with roots that reach deep into the water. Such trees are not bothered by the heat or worried by long months of drought" (Jeremiah 17:7–8).

CHOICE #4: PERSIST WITH PATIENCE

Healing rarely comes quickly. It frequently moves slowly, one baby step at a time. Sometimes our growth is barely perceptible. Sometimes it takes three steps forward and two steps back. Sometimes we feel stuck in neutral, wondering if anything will ever change.

The Western world of the twenty-first century is an impatient culture. We want things *now*. Instantaneously. Do you recall the personal computers of ten or fifteen years ago? We thought they were wonderful. Cutting edge. Did it ever occur to us that booting up a program or saving a document "took too long"? Are you kidding? It was only a matter of seconds. But if we went back to those machines now, the pauses and delays would drive us crazy. We're used to instant everything.

And when things don't happen as quickly as we think they should, we get angry. Or simply give up. In his powerful classic, *The Imitation of Christ*, Thomas á Kempis wrote, "All men commend patience although few are willing to practice it."

So true. And yet to grow and heal, we all need to learn patience. For no matter how hard we work, God is ultimately in control of life's agenda. As Peter Marshall prayed, "Teach us, O Lord, the disciplines of patience, for to wait is often harder than to work."

Emotional healing takes time. Dr. Thomas Whiteman gives us five reasons why time is so important:

- **Time gives you rest.** We all need downtime. In fact, when you push yourself too hard for too long, your body will eventually break down in some way.
- **Time enlarges your focus.** When wounded, your mind naturally constricts to focus on your own needs, your own feelings, and your own recovery. Over time you'll gain a more balanced perspective about your own needs and those of others.
- **Time helps you get all the facts.** Time helps you gain a truer understanding of yourself and your situation. With time you can get past the pain and start seeing the real issues.
- **Time lets you see how things turn out.** In the wake of trouble or trauma, we all tend to think the

future looks bleak. But over time the future often unfolds more brightly than we expect.

- **Time allows you to balance out your life.**
  After a while people realize their own imbalances. When a wound is fresh, it's easy to be too selfish, too serious, too frivolous, too lazy, too talkative, or too quiet.

As we recognize that time is just a part of healing, we can relax and be patient. When I first became a psychologist, this was one of my greatest frustrations. I wanted to give a formula and have everybody's wounds immediately disappear. Life doesn't work that way. In fact, my impatience made things worse. Now I know that healing is a process. No matter how much I push, pressure, or fume, it's almost always going to take more time than I think it should.

Patience is an act of faith. Once we risk, we must wait. David tells us to "be still in the presence of the LORD, and wait patiently for him to act.... Travel steadily along his path" (Psalm 37:7, 34). Impatience takes us nowhere positive. In fact it frequently increases our frustration and irritability, adding to our anger, fear, shame, and sorrow. Patience steps forward, trusting God to take us where He wants us, according to His schedule.

Patience never comes into our lives empty-handed; it always packs an armload of incomparable rewards, including wisdom, faith, and peace.

And did you know that Patience has a brother? His name is *Persistence*. Persistence simply refuses to give up. Patience waits; persistence waits and waits and waits. Great things take time to accomplish. Houses take time to build, books take time to write, seeds take time to grow and bloom into beautiful flowers. Calvin Coolidge said, "Nothing in the world can take the place of persistence." The determination to keep running the race when your sides ache and your legs are rubber is self-discipline in action. Persistence falls down five times, but stands up six.

As a young boy, Bruce Wayne fell down a deep, deserted well in the 2005 blockbuster movie, *Batman Begins*. Bruce was physically hurt and emotionally terrified. As his father carried him into the family house, he asked, "Why do we fall, Bruce?" But before his son could respond, he answered his own question: "So we can learn to pick ourselves up." That's the key to trusting again: learning how to pick ourselves up.

ANYTHING IS POSSIBLE

Once we've been wounded, we want to do whatever we can to keep from being wounded again. We grow wary and careful. Sometimes our worries keep us up all night, and sometimes our fears paralyze us during the day. We might avoid certain people or places or activities. Our wounds steal our innocence, and we often think we'll never trust as completely as before. If we're not careful, our wounds will shrink our world and its amazing possibilities.

The only way to grow is by learning to trust again.

I love the way Moses said, "Oh, that you would choose life" (Deuteronomy 30:19). That's what every wounded warrior needs. We need life.

Remember Kyle? Remember how he wanted to die when Lisa left him for Derek? During the next year he experienced every negative emotion possible, from anger and hatred to sorrow and shame. He spent many hours sitting in front of the television set feeling sorry for himself.

Then one morning he looked in the mirror and realized how pathetic he looked. He decided at that moment that he could either let his wound destroy him...or he could live life again.

So he brushed his teeth, shaved his face, and called some friends to meet for lunch. Over the next week he accepted his situation, let go of his hurt, and started taking risks again. On that day he chose to live and trust again.

Did his choice make the next day easier?

No. All of the pain and difficulties and anger came rushing back as he sat alone in his car and punched his dashboard.

But Kyle kept repeating his choice to move ahead, one day at a time. As the months passed, it *did* get easier. Yes, there were relapses. But for every relapse, Kyle would intentionally take another risk.

When Kyle met Kristi he was nervous. What if she didn't like him? What if he acted like a jerk? What if she hurt him? What if she was untrustworthy or unfaithful? They dated for two years, fell in love, and are now married. Kristi has adopted Kyle's two children, and this new family is happier than Kyle ever thought possible. If we asked Kyle today whether it was worth trusting again, he would smile and say, "If I hadn't risked trusting again, I would never have discovered how good God can be."

KIM LOVED BOTH OF HER PARENTS.

When she was nine, her parents' divorce was tearing her apart. Her heart was broken, and the pain was beyond words. She watched her father fall into a depression that only grew darker and darker. When it seemed as though life could get no worse, her father brutally killed her mother and then took his own life.

Kim's grief was more than she could handle; for days on end she could not stop crying. She moved in with her grandparents, who bought her a small horse to distract her from her wounds. Riding Firefly became Kim's refuge from a shattered life. Racing across the landscape, she rode so fast that her tears were blown from her eyes and her troubles were left behind. Over time Kim's wounds healed, and she married a wonderful man.

Then God gave Kim a dream.

He let her know that her story need not be wasted. She realized that a horse had saved her life and healed her wounds, so maybe the same could happen for other children. From her story came Crystal Peaks Youth Ranch, a nonprofit ranch that pairs neglected horses with children in pain to create a place of healing and hope.

A dark night can give way to a glorious sunrise. And a tragic wound can set the stage for a wonderful story. In a book entitled *Hope Rising,* Kim Meeder tells her story and the stories of children at her camp. On the last page of the book, she writes, "Like standing on a mountainous trail, we can *choose* which way to go.… When confronted by pain, we can *choose* to take the descending trail that most often leads to a dark and lonely place.… Or we can select the ascending trail and, with some effort and perseverance, we can *choose* to allow our pain to motivate us toward becoming better people, to move us toward a better place."

When we choose the ascending trail, we transform our pain into a promise of hope. The best way to do this is by telling our story.

SPEAKING OUT

Stories should not be hidden away. Your story is very important—a significant part of who you are. It can teach, encourage, and inspire others. It can change their lives.

When Jesus says, "Don't hide your light under a basket! Instead, put it on a stand and let it shine for all" (Matthew 5:15), He is talking about our lives. Our whole lives. The good and bad, the successes and failures, the beautiful and ugly. Throughout the Old Testament, we are told to remember what God has done. Asaph, one of the writers of the Psalms, declared,

> I recall all you have done, O LORD;
> I remember your wonderful deeds of long ago.
> They are constantly in my thoughts.
> I cannot stop thinking about them. (Psalm 77:11–12)

Not only did God's wonderful deeds inhabit this good man's thoughts; he also wrote them down as a way of telling others. And here we are some three thousand years later responding to those very words!

We all need to be prepared to tell our story at any time and in any place. It's amazing how sharing our hurts can break down walls between people. It connects us with others and opens hearts. Suddenly pride and pretense disappear. Two sharers become wounded travelers, together seeking God's grace and comfort.

It takes *courage* to tell our story, for we must expose our wounds and make ourselves vulnerable. It also takes *compassion*, for as our hearts break over the hurts of others, we yearn to somehow ease their pain; our story links us to *their* story and pain. We stand beside them unwrapping our wounds, dispelling a little of their isolation and loneliness. As Chuck Swindoll writes in *For Those Who Hurt*, "With God's arm firmly around my shoulders, I have the strength and stability to place my arm around another."

To speak out effectively, we must prepare. We need to think through what we want to say. Our story might answer the following questions:

- What is my wound?
- When did it happen?
- What did I feel?
- How did I respond?
- What did God do?
- What did I learn?

With these questions in mind we can continue to use our wounds to help others. We can make a difference.

Organizing our thoughts helps us to speak more clearly. And honesty is very important. Don't make your descriptions of events and experiences better or worse than they were. An honest story is frequently more powerful than a story perfectly told.

Here are a few hints about telling your story:

- Relax.
- Keep it simple.
- Make it short.
- Be real.
- Answer their questions.
- Share what you have learned.

- Show hope.
- Encourage at every opportunity.

As a psychologist, I listen to people's stories all day long. I love my job, and I love hearing these stories. They touch my heart and stretch my faith. I wish everybody could hear the stories of searching and struggle that I have heard.

Stories change lives. But only if they are told.

Lori, the oldest of three sisters, grew up in a strong Christian home. But at twenty-one, she found herself single and pregnant. Afraid to tell anyone, she went alone to a clinic one cold December morning and had an abortion.

A year later Lori came to my office, filled with guilt and shame, to tell her story. We spoke of forgiveness and freedom. But when I suggested passing her story along to someone else, Lori was too frightened.

Two years had passed when Lana came to my office. She was the middle child of three sisters. She grew up in a strong Christian family, but at twenty found herself single and pregnant. Afraid to tell anyone, she went alone to a clinic one April morning and had an abortion. We spoke of forgiveness and healing. Lana also was too frightened to share her story with anyone, especially with her family.

Another two years had passed when Lucy came to my office. She was the baby of three sisters. At twenty-one she found herself single and pregnant. Unable to identify anyone who would understand, she went alone to a clinic and had an abortion. We spoke of forgiveness, and I encouraged her to talk to her older sisters.

She told me that Lori and Lana would never understand. They were perfect sisters and would reject her for bringing disgrace on the family.

My heart broke. Three wounded sisters, each unknowingly withholding from the others the encouragement and comfort that they all needed so much. As far as I know, not one of these three has yet found the courage to share her story with the others. How terribly sad!

THE SEVEN S'S

Telling your story takes determination and humility. The Chinese Christian, Watchman Nee, wrote, "You can only help others in proportion to what you yourself have suffered. The greater the price, the more you can help others. The lesser the price, the less you can help others." So I urge you to enthusiastically embrace your pain and seriously consider each of the following steps:

We need to stop.

It's easy to keep quiet and bury our pain deep in our hearts. Fear of rejection or embarrassment may reinforce our silence. But years of working with men and women in crisis has convinced me that wounds carefully hidden away end up hurting more.

For one thing, how can anyone offer comfort if we've hidden our pain from others? In fact, our silence is often selfish, for we can easily become more concerned with protecting ourselves than with helping others. Each of us has a powerful story about how we have dealt with difficult situations. We have learned lessons, developed insights, and gained perspective. To keep quiet about these is to waste your pain. We need to stop being silent.

We need to stand up.

We need to admit our wounds. Since we all have our hurts and hurdles, we need to stop pretending all is well and stand up to the truth. My friend Tim struggled with rejection and failure. Yet as he worked through it, he told me he *had* to tell others. He said, "It was really hard for me to come clean and talk about my hurt, but I wanted to help someone else out there."

It takes courage to stand up and speak out, but one person's sharing encourages others to do the same. Soon we are not alone, and the negative cycle of hopelessness, helplessness, and despair can be broken.

We need to search.

We are surrounded by people who may be struggling. But we are either so busy, distracted, or self-absorbed that we don't notice those right in front of us who are in pain. Sometimes, perhaps, we do notice. But we don't know what to do or say, so we ignore them.

Most people dealing with pain leave little clues…for anyone who might be caring enough to notice. Some of the clues are intentional, like sad comments, sighs, frowns, tears, or maybe just staring out a window. Other clues are unintentional, but every bit as clear—such as the dark circles under the eyes, the distractedness, the sagging shoulders.

We need to search, actively looking and listening, for those who yearn for our encouragement. Then we can reach out and let them know they are not alone. People need to know they are valued and appreciated, especially when they find themselves trapped in the vortex of their suffering.

We need to speak.

Some people open their hearts easily; others struggle to find the right words. Part of what adds meaning and purpose to our wounds is to be able to communicate to others at least some of what we have endured.

Charles Spurgeon wrote, "I could go to the deeps a hundred times to cheer a downcast spirit. It is good for me to have been afflicted, that I might know how to speak a word in season to one that is weary."

Our words, whether written, spoken, or sung, can give hope and encouragement to anyone who hears them, but especially to those still struggling.

We need to serve.

Volunteering to help people in difficult situations provides a nonverbal means of providing support and care. Service is love in action. It allows us to give, just as others gave to us in our time of desperation. (It may also open up opportunities for us to tell our story.) To help others in whatever way we can is an affirmation that our wounds did not sideline or destroy us. Instead, our wounds made and defined us. Our wounds shape us into better servants.

Action gives our pain meaning. As we serve others in desperate situations, we take the light our pain has ignited and use it to lead others through their darkness. Our difficulties suddenly become a gift that needs to be shared, not wasted. Our service not only benefits others—it also strengthens us. As a young man told me today, "I got so concerned with helping others, that I forgot to be afraid."

We need to smile.

Who can overestimate the power of a smile and a positive attitude to infuse a struggling soul with hope? When others hear our story and see that we can be upbeat and hopeful in spite of the pain, we give them something to hold onto. What a powerful influence for good!

Picture a dreary, overcast afternoon. Suddenly the clouds part for an instant and a shaft of sunlight illumines a forest path or turns a rain-wet street into molten gold. That's what a genuine, warm greeting, a light heart, and a positive attitude can become for someone in the grip of discouragement. We become proof of light beyond the darkness. Wounded people feel as though their pain will never end. They see a desolate landscape and believe that it goes on forever.

But a simple smile, a heart strengthened with hope in God—these encourage the hopeless to keep their chin up and to keep on fighting.

We need to show.

Show the world that most of our limits are in our mind. With God's help we can do things we thought would be impossible. When David was in trouble he wrote, "In your strength I can crush an army; with my God I can scale any wall" (Psalm 18:29). No mere army, no looming wall of stone could dampen this man's confidence. His eyes were upon the Lord, and he believed in the God of the impossible.

Let those who are struggling know that wounds are a poor excuse for abandoning objectives and dreams. Yes, certain goals may need to be adjusted and timetables may need to be expanded, but wounds need not be a road to failure or second best. Ironically, it's often our wounds that fuel us with a greater drive to aim for higher goals—greater drive and higher goals than those of people who've never been badly hurt.

So show your success. Then challenge and coach others to turn their dreams into reality.

These seven elements are guidelines by which we can all boldly tell our stories and impact the lives of our hearers.

Each of us has a wonderful story, though it may have its moments of pain, sorrow, struggle, anger, guilt, grief, confusion, and desperation. We must let our story be told; we must shout if from the rooftops and let it echo throughout our community.

We must tell our friends and children. We must speak about it at home, at work, and wherever we go. We must never let our story be wasted.

A CRISIS AND A VICTORY

Dave was ready for battle. The Vietcong had tried to sink his four-man patrol boat on the narrow Van Lo Tay River in Vietnam. The firefight was fierce but brief as thirteen B-40 antitank rockets flew all around him. Dave sat behind his 50-caliber machine gun, sweeping the shore with bullets. In the midst of the fight Dave took some shrapnel to the face. The boat captain pulled back to camp for medical attention and additional ammo.

Dave's injury was only minor, so twelve hours later he was back on the river for a predawn patrol. The men were assigned the task of finding the bunker that had shot at them and taking it out. As their boat drew close, the early morning hour made it too dark to see. Dave threw a phosphorous grenade toward the bunker, but it didn't provide quite enough light. As he started to throw a second grenade, it went off in his hand. The explosion stripped the skin off the right side of his head and neck, his right shoulder, the right half of his chest, and both arms. In that instant Dave lost 40 percent of his skin and sixty pounds of flesh. He was twenty-two years old and mutilated beyond recognition.

It took the doctors fourteen months to put Dave back together, and the pain was excruciating. Scars covered practically his entire body. Yet Dave Roever would not give up. Through this tragedy he discovered that God will not let us down. As others encouraged him, he learned to encourage others. Soon Dave was speaking all over the world, sharing his story about hope and healing. He used his wounds and scars to reach out.

"Scars don't just disappear on their own," Dave wrote in the book *Nobody's Ever Cried for Me.* "Somewhere you have to stop and get involved. You've got to cry with them, hold them, stop giving advice and listen." So Dave listens and tells his story hundreds of times every year at churches, high schools, military installations, and business conventions. In fact, he has spoken face to face with almost six million students. His story has changed thousands of lives, giving those who felt hopeless a new and exciting outlook.

Dave Roever has fought the good fight, winning many a difficult battle, and is helping others do the same. In 2003, thirty-four years after his injuries, the Department of the Navy gave Dave a Purple Heart for his service.

Dave Roever is a hero. But that was true long before he received a medal.

HIS LIFE WAS FINISHED.

He sat in his room and stared hopelessly at the wall. He was so low, his wife wondered if he'd ever recover. Nothing had gone right in the previous three years.

He'd lost all his money in the stock market.

His career had collapsed.

He was hit by a car, leaving him in chronic pain.

Yet Winston Churchill rallied his optimism and refused to give up. As England faced certain war, Churchill stepped up to the challenge. In his first speech as Prime Minister, he vowed "to wage war until victory is won." For Churchill this determination did not come easily; it was an intentional, determined act of will. Though his wounds triggered depression, self-doubt, and discouragement, he would not allow these to crush him. When his nation needed him most, Churchill told the British people, "We shall not flag or fail. We shall go on to the end.... We shall fight on the beaches, we shall fight on the landing grounds, we shall fight in the fields and in the streets, we shall fight in the hills. We shall never surrender!"

Life is an amazing adventure, full of excitement and discouragement, sweet dreams and wicked nightmares, smooth waters and turbulent storms. We wish that all would be bright, people would always be kind, and wounds would fade from our thoughts like an old fairy tale.

This is not reality.

And in all probability, it wouldn't even be healthy.

Maybe we need some pain.

Ann Bradstreet suggests, "If we had no winter, the spring would not be so pleasant." I know that when my wife Tami is gone with girlfriends to the beach for a weekend, I appreciate her more when she returns. We tend to value more what we have when we can contrast it with times of difficulty. Our wounds help us appreciate our blessings.

Hurts and hurdles surround us. We resent them and fight against them.

But what if wounds were a means of moving us forward?

What if pain was a teacher and difficulties were opportunities?

What if a life without struggle was a wasted life?

When Pope John Paul II was shot by a Bulgarian assassin, he saw the situation as a chance to model forgiveness. On the one-year anniversary of the attempted murder he said, "In the designs of Providence there are no mere coincidences."

A wound may be a blessed event, if only we embrace the blessing and don't bog down in the agony and distress. We are not minimizing the suffering; we're only saying that it may have a meaning that shines through the darkness. Difficult as it may be right now for you to affirm this, the pain may be worth it. Brennan Manning writes in *The Rabbi's Heartbeat*, "Hope knows that if great trials are avoided, great deeds remain undone and the possibility of growth into greatness of soul is aborted."

Troubles happen, but life moves on. We either move forward with it or we relive it, focusing over and over again on our difficulty. We all must ask ourselves, *Am I living life in my rearview mirror or with my eyes intently focused on the road ahead?*

Focusing only on the past stunts our growth. It entangles us in the most negative emotions of our past. Everything stops. The apostle Paul wrote, "One thing I do: Forgetting what is behind and straining toward what is ahead, I press on toward the goal to win the prize for which God has called me heavenward in Christ Jesus" (Philippians 3:13–14, NIV).

We all need to push forward; that's where *life is.* We must start by stepping out. David Livingstone insisted, "I will go anywhere as long as it is forward."

After surviving a 220-foot suicide jump off the Golden Gate Bridge, Kevin Himes, age eighteen, realized he really didn't want to die. A priest visited him in the hospital and said, "You are a miracle. Now go out and save lives." Kevin took that challenge seriously, and now he speaks to young people about depression and suicide. He shares his story. "I was blessed. I was given a second chance," says Kevin. Now he's telling people to not give up, to move forward, to live life to the fullest.

STEPPING OUT

"My dream," said ten-year-old Lydia, whose father had died suddenly, "is that next year will be better than this year."

That's what stepping out is all about. It's expecting something better, rather than letting anxiety hold you back. Bill and Gloria Gaither summed it up when they wrote, "Because He lives, I can face tomorrow."

Christ gives us strength and comfort and hope. Regardless of the past, He will be with us as we move forward.

Scripture tells us Jesus was "a man of sorrows, acquainted with bitterest grief" (Isaiah 53:3). Jesus understands pain. He suffered so we could be healed and forgiven. He paved a way so we could have a bright tomorrow. Isaiah 53 tells us that He was...

despised

rejected

weighed down

wounded

crushed

beaten

whipped

oppressed

treated harshly.

Anybody who saw the violence and brutality of Mel Gibson's movie *The Passion of the Christ* couldn't help but be moved by Jesus' torment on His last day. What makes it so powerful is that He did it for us.

God has great dreams for us. All we need to do is step out and grasp them. With God, we are all bigger than our wounds—maybe even bigger *because* of our wounds. Paul wrote to the church of Galatia, "Christ has set us free to live a free life. So take your stand! Never again let anyone put a harness of slavery on you" (Galatians 5:1, The Message).

What wonderful counsel! God has set us free—free from our wounds, our guilt, our fears, and our past. We can move forward with confidence and enthusiasm, confident that God is with us and enthusiastic that He has marvelous plans in store for us. Somebody once said, "The shadow will always be behind you, if you walk toward the light." Walking toward the light means stepping out and not letting anything stop us. God is waiting for us; all we need is the courage and faith to join Him.

Our future will not be perfect. There will be new challenges, new difficulties, and yes, new wounds. But we will be stronger for what we have gone through. Louisa May Alcott wrote, "I am not afraid of storms, for I am learning how to sail my ship."

It's interesting that she didn't say that she *had learned* to sail, but that she *was learning*. We are all in process; none of us has arrived. Yet on this journey, with God's help and our determination, we move forward and discover victory.

Wounds are a part of life. When they hit, we may yell and cry, but in the end they strengthen us if we let them. Phillips Brooks encourages us, "Do not pray for easy lives, pray to be stronger men." John Donne was pastor of the largest church in London during a period in the early 1600s when one-third of the city died of the plague. When he was told he had this terrible disease and he had little time left, Donne refused to give up. He faced his pain and cried out to God, "Batter my heart...bend your force to break, blow, burn and make me new." John Donne marched forward and lived another seven years, encouraging, preaching, and walking with God.

Pain changes us, but it need not make us bitter. Pain can make us the best we can be. Paul writes that "when we have trouble or calamity, when we are hunted down or destroyed...if we are hungry, or penniless, or in danger" God has not deserted us. "Despite all this, overwhelming victory is ours" (Romans 8:35–37, TLB). This is what Noble Alexander discovered, even though he was imprisoned in Cuba for twenty-two years. He wrote, "In spite of the painful reflections and memories, I have no time for bitterness. My life is filled with too much happiness, too many loving, caring people to allow myself to be devoured by the cancer of hate.

I rejoice. I sing. I laugh. I celebrate, because I know that my God reigns supreme."

THANKING GOD

It's initially difficult to thank God for our struggles and pain. We want to get angry and ask Him, *Why?*

Sometimes He answers that question.

But not very often.

There are other questions He is much more likely to answer, like…

What? *What is this all about, Lord? What do You want me to learn, to see, to do?*

How? *How am I to endure this? How will I make it through? How will I get through these dark waters without drowning? How do You want to use this in my life?*

But when it comes to questions such as *When?* or *Why?*, we probably shouldn't expect a definitive answer. The timings of life are in His hands (see Psalm 31:15). And we may never know why—at least not until we pass beyond this fragile life and see our Maker face to face. Maybe it's important that we don't know all the details about the whys of our suffering; then we'd lose one important opportunity for faith. It's in trusting God, through the easy and the difficult, that we grow close to Him. And the closer we draw to Him, the easier it is to thank Him for all things.

Gratitude reshapes our attitude, making even the tough times positive. In his book *Now That I Have Cancer, I am Whole,* John

Robert McFarland writes, "I'm so grateful I never have bad days. I have nauseated days and frightened days. Tired days and hurting days. Long days and short days. Silent days and alone days...cold days and warm days. But no bad days. I'm so grateful."

Thankfulness keeps us focused on the positive. It reminds us that there is always hope and that difficulties will pass. Wounds have their limits, but thankfulness doesn't. In fact, the greater our gratitude, the more we become aware that we're healed and that Jesus is truly the ultimate physician.

Gratitude is faith in action. Every moment of every day is full of reasons to be thankful. Randy Stonehill writes, "Celebrate each heartbeat." Gratitude makes us more alive, more enthusiastic, more optimistic. Gratitude is a prism that adds bright colors and twinkling lights to everything we see. In our darkest nights, it is a beacon that guides us to our heavenly Father.

As Dr. Gregory Jantz writes, "Finding God-given blessings in every hour of distress is one of the most important keys to bouncing back, being resilient, and becoming strong again."

There are millions of things to thank God for; we are only limited by our poor attention, narrow perspective, and lack of faith. David marveled as he pondered God's goodness and care, writing, "How precious it is, Lord, to realize that you are thinking about me constantly! I can't even count how many times a day your thoughts turn toward me. And when I waken in the morning, you are still thinking of me!" (Psalm 139:17–18, TLB).

But as we journey through times of trouble, there are two things in particular that we need to thank Him for.

First, let's thank God for *our wounds*.

They are gifts, and at the same time, tests. Helen Keller wrote, "I thank God for my handicaps for, through them, I have found myself, my work, and my God."

Second, let's thank God for *His presence*.

He is always right beside us, even when we don't feel His arm around our shoulders. The prophet Isaiah recognized God as "a refuge for the needy in his distress, a shelter from the storm and a shade from the heat" (Isaiah 25:4, NIV). He has played these roles for each of us, and we need to thank Him. Not because He needs our gratitude, but because we need to give it. Thanking God makes all things worthwhile.

EMBRACING ETERNITY

This life is not all there is. At its very best, in the sweetest and most sublime of moments, it is only a brief glimpse at an unimaginably beautiful world beyond our physical senses. This life is shorter than we realize, but eternity is longer than we can imagine. Randy Alcorn, founder of Eternal Perspective Ministries, pictures our life as a small dot on an infinite line. Moses writes, "Seventy years are given to us! Some may even reach eighty. But even the best of these years are filled with pain and trouble; soon they disappear, and we are gone" (Psalm 90:10).

That is when our real life begins.

What we currently experience is simply a foretaste, a warm-up, a shadow, a prologue to the real thing. Beyond this life is a land called heaven which has no tears, no troubles, no suffering, no wounds. It is a world where everything is healed and nothing is broken. This is the land where we belong. As Abraham Lincoln said, "Man was made for eternity."

Our wounds make us more willing to let go of what we have here. Our trials and troubles cause us to look forward to a better, more glorious world. Peter explains that "we are looking forward to the new heavens and new earth he has promised" (2 Peter 3:13).

Our sufferings and struggles make us impatient for an eternity unmarred by the painful realities we face daily. Francis DeSales wrote, "We will soon be in eternity and then we will see how all the affairs of the world are such little things."

Living in the light of eternity places everything in perspective. It gives our days new meaning and causes us to reassess what matters most. Eternity points out our foolishness and plants a peace in our hearts that defies current circumstances. Looking forward *draws* us forward. It constantly reminds us that Matthew Henry was right when he said, "It ought to be the business of every day to prepare for our last day." But let me add: "...and for all the days of eternity."

Life is full of challenges! Why this fact surprises so many people is baffling. Some people appear to have light burdens while others have overwhelming challenges. As Rick Warren writes, "Life on earth is a test." Each and every difficulty is a test to determine our patience, courage, character, determination, and faith. Sometimes we handle our challenges well; sometimes we don't. The apostle James reminds us that "God blesses the people who patiently endure testing. Afterward they will receive the crown of life that God has promised to those who love him" (James 1:12).

As we each learn to deal with our wounds, our perspective on this world improves and our appreciation of the next increases. In heaven we will gain incomprehensibly amazing rewards based on how we pass the tests in this life. Yet, because of God's grace, even if we don't pass earth's tests, eternity will still be full of joy, radiance, and transcendent beauty. D. L. Moody said, "Take courage. We walk in the wilderness today and the promised land tomorrow."

UNQUENCHABLE FAITH

We all wish life were a playground, but the Bible tells us it's a battleground. We get tackled, beat-up, and wounded. Even so, through it all our faith grows. And as our faith grows, we draw closer and closer to God.

Paul tells us, "In every battle you will need faith as your shield" (Ephesians 6:16). Several years later he wrote, "Endure hardship with us like a good soldier" (2 Timothy 2:3, NIV). In the battlegrounds of life, our faith has the potential to grow stronger and deeper. Our wounds become symbols of our fight. They are nothing for which to feel ashamed or insecure. In God's eyes there is nothing wrong with our wounds.

Life is tough and the answers are not easy. There are no magic formulas or quick cures for our wounds, but there is hope in the midst of our pain. There is meaning in every tragedy, even though the meaning may be cloudy. Chuck Colson recently wrote, "I don't have to make sense of the agonies I bear or hear a clear answer. God is not a creature of my emotions or senses…. I can only cling to the certainty that he is and he has spoken." God is calling us and He is always leading us somewhere.

Difficulties are opportunities to move forward. They can bring out the best or the worst in us, depending on how we see them and what we do with them. Troubles transform us, if we let them. As we've said before, challenges can empower us and take us to the next level. God doesn't want to hurt us, but He is willing to use our pain to accomplish great things in us and around us. Zane Grey, the famous Western novelist, once wrote that his recipe for greatness was "to bear up under loss, to fight the bitterness of defeat and the weakness of grief, to be a victor over anger, to smile when tears are close…to look up with unquenchable faith in something ever more about to be."

This is what I want: an unquenchable faith.

Without wounds, my faith remains untested. And unless I move forward, my faith will remain unrewarded.

In the end, we must never forget that God loves us. He yearns to heal our wounds when the time is right. He is waiting to comfort us as soon as we ask Him. He is eager to strengthen us as we lean more and more on Him.

So as we walk this trouble-filled world, let us hold firmly to His joy, His peace, His purpose, and especially His hope. For it is through hope that we march forward, and it is in marching forward that we discover that God can meet our every need.